I0057215

Fire, Water, Earth, Air, and Data

Mobilizing Data with Keys, Models, and Governance

Blair Kjenner

Kewal Dhariwal

With contributions by William (Bill) Inmon

Technics Publications

TECHNICS PUBLICATIONS

TECHNOLOGY / LEADERSHIP

115 Linda Vista
Sedona, AZ 86336 USA
https://www.TechnicsPub.com

Edited by Sadie Hoberman
Cover design by Lorena Molinari

All rights reserved. No part of this book may be reproduced or transmitted in any form or by any means, electronic or mechanical, including photocopying, recording or by any information storage and retrieval system, without written permission from the publisher, except for brief quotations in a review.

The authors and publisher have taken care in the preparation of this book but make no expressed or implied warranty of any kind and assume no responsibility for errors or omissions. No liability is assumed for incidental or consequential damages in connection with or arising out of the use of the information or programs contained herein.

All trade and product names are trademarks, registered trademarks, or service marks of their respective companies and are the property of their respective holders and should be treated as such.

First Printing 2022

Copyright © 2022 by Blair Kjenner and Kewal Dhariwal

ISBN, print ed.   9781634628792
ISBN, Kindle ed. 9781634628808
ISBN, ePub ed.   9781634628815
ISBN, PDF ed.   9781634628822

Library of Congress Control Number: 2022943120

Acknowledgments

I would sincerely like to thank Kewal Dhariwal for his support throughout the journey of bringing this book to fruition. I have a tremendous amount of respect for Kewal's knowledge and experience in delivering education, corporate training, building international standards, and constructing innovative applications development and certification over the past 40 years.

Along with Kewal, I want to thank Bill Inmon (the father of Data Warehousing and streaming data analytics) for his input, foreword, data warehousing and analytics, and for his guidance.

I would also like to thank my wife who also provided continuous support. Once again, without her support, I could have never completed this project.

Finally, I would like to thank simon crossley, Bob Gray, and Rene Kohut for their efforts in reviewing the book and providing comments. You helped to make this book a better product.

Contents at a Glance

Contents

Foreword

*The mind, once stretched by a new idea, never
returns to its original dimensions.*

Ralph Waldo Emerson

There comes a time when a new idea emerges, and once shared, that idea will permeate the whole industry. This was so when we first coined the term *data warehousing* in Calgary.

The authors of this book are now sharing with you ideas that will greatly impact how we architect and integrate three-dimensional (3D) enterprise systems for the future.

They have programmed and developed systems for almost every imaginable organization—healthcare, manufacturing, production and mining companies, professional associations, governments, and nonprofits. They have learned and overcome many challenges when faced with developing very large enterprise systems.

Data is an essential element of all applications. I encourage you to explore the new ideas, concepts, architectures, taxonomies, and ontologies that this book offers you as a way to progress our industry towards high-quality data and 3D enterprise systems integration.

William (Bill) Inmon

Introduction

Imagine if enterprise system (ES) architects were assigned a project to create an enterprise system for all business entities within a large government organization. This includes its departments, boards, commissions, and its healthcare entities.

The system's goal is that every business entity within the government must be able to address all of their operational and financial needs. Furthermore, the system must ensure that data is only entered once and then shared securely between business entities. The new system must allow data from all business entities to be easily aggregated for reporting, data warehousing, business intelligence, data analytics, machine learning (ML), and artificial intelligence (AI). The new system must also be maintainable. It should allow features to be created and shared among business entities. Business entities should be able to easily take these functions and modify them to meet their unique needs.

Undoubtedly, this government would benefit significantly if such a system could be created affordably. The government would be highly efficient because it would eliminate all the work associated with keying data from one system to the next and then reconciling against spreadsheets. Furthermore, all the technical work related to trying to aggregate data between systems would be significantly reduced since the system would encompass data from all business entities. Also, imagine how the government could leverage ML/AI because all data is neatly organized across all business entities.

As much as I hope you would see this type of enterprise system would be of value, you probably recognize that this would be an insurmountable challenge. Based on our current approach to enterprise systems and the need to share data between business entities, it would push architects toward creating a single monolithic system with a single database.

But, of course, creating a single monolithic system of this size would surely fail. That does not mean that such a need does not exist. We know organizations should not be forced to key data from one system to the next and then reconcile this data. Furthermore, we should be able to aggregate data from many business entities for reporting and ML/AI. The need for mobilizing data so it can be shared between systems and aggregated for reporting, warehousing, and analytics is growing every day with the promised benefits of ML/AI.

The challenge with ML/AI is the amount of effort the IT industry spends on collecting and cleansing data.

According to Dataversity.net, 80% of the effort for
AI is related to collecting and cleansing data.[1]

This statistic speaks volumes about the flaws in our current approach to ESs. The challenge of collecting and cleansing data increases exponentially based on the number of systems. Large organizations can have hundreds or even thousands of systems to address all their business needs. In the context of this book, an enterprise system includes enterprise resources planning (ERP), customer relationship management (CRM), and supply chain management (SCM) packages.

Certainly, large enterprise resource planning (ERP) vendors have helped reduce the number of systems within an organization. Still, no ERP vendor so far has taken on this newly imagined scope mentioned above. We believe the industry hasn't matured sufficiently to provide these new integration methods. It's more likely that the task of reconstructing a SAP, MS Dynamics, or PeopleSoft may be onerous, expensive, and risky.

We wrote this book to empower you to create enterprise systems of the magnitude mentioned above. The new

---

[1]   https://www.dataversity.net/survey-shows-data-scientists-spend-time-cleaning-data/.

system is called a three-dimensional enterprise system (3D ES).

The current paradigm for creating enterprise systems is one-dimensional. In that dimension, architects create systems in isolation based on their preferences. When we attempt to integrate them with other systems, we discover it is difficult and costly. The more systems to integrate, the more the costs escalate. The new paradigm has three dimensions - Data, System, and Time:

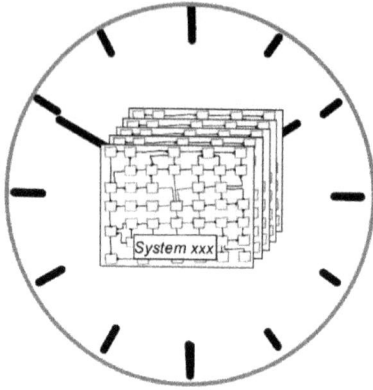

- The data dimension (illustrated by the data model page on the image above) manages data to meet the unique needs of business entities.

- The system dimension (illustrated by many different data model pages, each with a unique system id) allows us to easily aggregate data from many different systems into a single system for reporting.

- The time dimension (illustrated by the clock in the image above) allows organizations to see how data changes over time as a result of built-in features for managing temporal (time-sensitive) data.

3D ESs will empower large organizations to aggregate data from all their business entities and see how that data changes over time. Data will only ever be entered once and shared many times. Common functionality will be created and then shared across business entities.

3D ESs will also address the needs of small organizations. It will allow them to adapt common functionality to meet their unique needs. Small organizations can exchange data with their customers, suppliers, and partners.

The goal to create such an architecture is certainly a stretch goal for the industry but one that is definitely needed. This book takes the first step toward achieving this goal.

My name is Blair Kjenner. I have designed and built ESs for forty years. My impetus to architect 3D ESs began when I took over a project management role for a project underway in the Alberta government for several years. By the time I got involved, the specifications were done, the technologies were selected, and development was underway. The project involved creating a central registry system that needed to integrate with systems within and outside the department. All the other systems we integrated with were custom systems as well.

When a team creates a custom system, I observed they follow the same basic process:

a. Define the requirements - involves documenting all requirements that are within scope.

b. Select a technology - involves selecting a technology stack based on the latest technologies available and department standards.

c. Develop an application framework - involves designing a user interface and creating an application framework to support it.

d. Develop the system and create the database - involves creating a system using the application framework. In the process a database is created that is unique as a fingerprint.

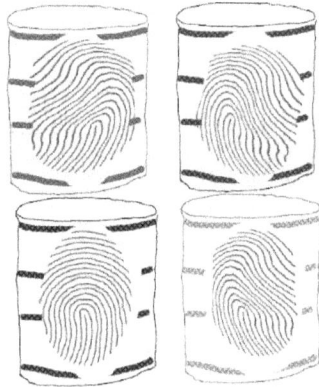

e. Attempt to integrate it – involves trying to create integrations with other systems only to figure out limited integrations can be accomplished.

Once the system is implemented, the support team assumes responsibility, where almost all of the system costs lie over the system's life.[2] In the early days of the system, the developers are easy to hire because they tend to like to work with the latest technologies. However, as the system ages, the technology will be deemed as dated, and support resources will be harder to find that want to work with the technology. When the technology becomes too dated, the team will create a business case to rewrite the system, and the cycle begins again. The challenge with rewriting the system is that the subject matter experts get drawn back into the process of creating the application, which consumes the time of the most valuable resources.

Another major issue is the duplication of effort that exists for creating systems. There are hundreds of features that are common to ES's that get recreated in each ES system. One example is functionality to authenticate users and then limit access to functions and data based on their privileges in every ES that gets created. This makes it challenging to upgrade all systems with a common feature. For example, if you needed to upgrade all the systems with a new authentication protocol, development teams would need to repeat this task with each system, with little functionality shared from one system to the next.

---

[2] "Frequently Forgotten Fundamental Facts about Software Engineering" by Robert L. Glass, (an article in IEEE Software May/June 2001).

When you look at the user's experience, they will often find they need to re-key data from one system to the next and then heavily rely on spreadsheets to reconcile and report on data.

The project with the government certainly inspired me to think about how to do things better, but the real inspiration came when I got involved in a project to help an oil and gas company find missing revenues. This involved reverse engineering the systems and then creating a reporting engine to compare data from one system to the next. In the end, we uncovered discrepancies between the same data in different systems, which resulted in many millions in missed revenues. The root cause was the lack of integration between systems, which resulted in overly complex business processes that forced users to re-key the same data update in multiple systems.

One of the key differences between this project and the government environment was the systems were primarily off-the-shelf package systems, like ERPs or "Best of Breed" packages (as opposed to custom-built systems in the government environment). It did not matter, though, because the same process exists for creating package systems as for custom systems. Namely, a development team will design and develop a system in a silo that will have a database that follows no standards.

Organizations struggle to integrate package systems to a large degree, just like we struggled to integrate custom systems. In the end, organizations are left with a hodgepodge of disparate systems that do not integrate, forcing them to re-key data from one system to the next and then heavily relying on spreadsheets to reconcile and report data between systems.

The project for the oil and gas company resulted in our team finding millions of dollars in missed revenues while exposing a highly inefficient administration process. This particular organization continued to spend a million dollars per month on their disparate systems and ended up with a hodgepodge of systems that could not integrate.

This was the breaking bad[3] point for me. It has become accepted business practice to rekey data from one system to the next and then reconcile with spreadsheets. As an industry, we need to do better for our clients. We need to be able to create affordable systems that have an inherent capability to mobilize data.

[3] Urban dictionary defines breaking bad as - Sometimes, life forces you to cross the line. Some call it "reaching the breaking point"; others call it "breaking bad."

One of the ways the industry has tried to do this is to engage a large ES/ERP vendor to automate more of the business in a single integrated system. ES vendors have had amazing success at helping large organizations reduce the number of disparate systems. Even so, here are some significant issues with implementing large ESs:

- ESs rarely eliminate all (or even most) of the disparate systems. These highly specialized package systems can still be necessary to address functionality not included in the larger ES.

- ESs can miss functionality that is needed, which means the system must be customized.

- The more an organization customizes its ES, the more it will struggle with upgrading the ES when new versions are released.

- If the ES is implemented in the cloud, the organization's IT team may not have access to the underlying database. This makes it difficult and increases the cost for its team to integrate the system with other systems or extract data to a data warehouse. It also makes it difficult for organizations to switch vendors.

- The organization that implements an ES can become dependent on the ES vendor or implementer with little ability to change.

- ESs can cost hundreds of millions and even billions of dollars to implement. This can represent a significant risk to the organization, mainly if the project goes over budget or fails completely.

So clearly, existing ESs have some significant drawbacks. At this point, we have only talked about trying to address the issues of a large organization. The hypothetical project described above is related to addressing the needs of all companies, including conglomerates.

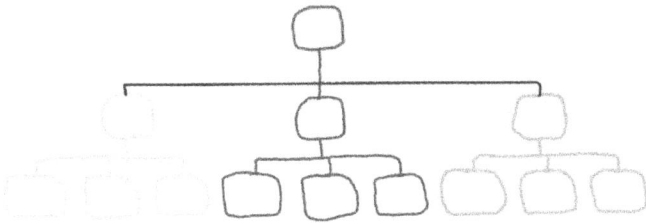

In the context of this book, a conglomerate is a group of interrelated business entities that work together as an organization to achieve a common goal. Here are examples of conglomerates:

- International businesses with business entities in each country.

- Government agencies consisting of departments, boards, and commissions.

- Healthcare entities like hospitals, clinics, labs, and funding bodies.

- Associations and unions with regional entities that all report to a main entity.

- Automobile manufacturers, suppliers, and dealerships.

- Oil and gas companies, suppliers, and regulators.

Ideally, with conglomerates, each entity should have a fully functional ES that they can customize to meet their unique needs. The ESs for all entities should be integrated to exchange data between entities and easily roll up data from the lowest level entities to the main entity.

Our ability to create an ES for conglomerates is poor at best.

Our only solution in the current paradigm is to create a monolithic system and then build controls so that one entity cannot view another entity's data. The solution gets further complicated when customizing the system to meet the unique needs of each entity.

The more the monolithic system grows in complexity, the greater the cost and higher the risk. Unfortunately, the costs increase exponentially as we add new features and scope to the system. It is not uncommon for monolithic systems to reach budgets of more than a billion dollars.

One example of a system that cost more than a billion dollars to implement was the health records system for the Alberta Government in Canada. This system was a central health records system that was accessible by all healthcare providers in the province. This system had a projected budget of 1.6 billion, according to an article in the Edmonton Journal on September 29, 2017.[4] To put a budget of 1.6 billion dollars into perspective, it is equivalent to hiring 2,000 full-time resources over a five-year period at a rate of $80 per hour.

Although the health records system was an excellent improvement to the healthcare system, it did not have capabilities for doing anything else for the healthcare entities other than allowing them to access personal health data securely. It did not help them manage their finance and administration or help them with their billing. All it did was add one more system to the mix of systems they had for operating their business. The budget would have been much larger to achieve a complete vision.

How can a system cost more than a billion dollars to create? It all has to do with the number of features.

---

[4] http://edmontonjournal.com/news/local-news/alberta-health-services-signs-459-million-deal-for-massive-new-technology-system.

From a simplistic view, it would be easy to believe that a system that deals with ten thousand features is ten times more costly than one that deals with a thousand features. Unfortunately, that is not correct. When you add a new feature to a system, you need to consider how that feature interacts with the existing features.

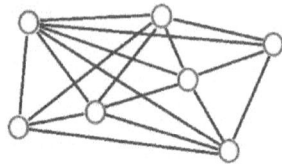

It is easy to assess the impact if it is a small system. However, it is not easy if the system has thousands of features. For example, if you expand the address component for a system from capturing just zip codes to also capturing a postal code, on the surface, it seems quite simple. It would be if the system only captures addresses and does nothing else. But if the system contains a shipping module that calculates shipping fees and product fees based on zip code, then the impact is much bigger. The larger the system, the more things can be impacted when adding a new feature.

Very often with monolithic systems, you often may not fully know the impact of a new feature until you reach acceptance testing or, worse yet, production. If a new feature causes another feature to fail, we report it as a bug. Fixing that bug can create more challenges. When we fix those bugs, additional bugs appear.

Adding more resources to the project only worsens the problem because now you must have that many more resources (people) that fully understand how all the features in the system relate to each other. Communication is a large task at the best of times, but with international teams and multiple languages and cultures, the task is much more difficult.

Eventually, the project fails because the team can never deliver a product that addresses all requirements.

To illustrate this in a different way, consider a pinball machine where each post represents the system's features. Adding a new feature to the system is like adding a post to the pinball machine and then firing a ball into the machine. Each time the ball hits a post, the cost of the system goes up by one thousand dollars. Firing the ball into a pinball machine with five posts drops out the bottom with minimal impact. If you fire it into a pinball machine with a thousand posts, the ball seemingly never drops out the bottom of the pinball machine.

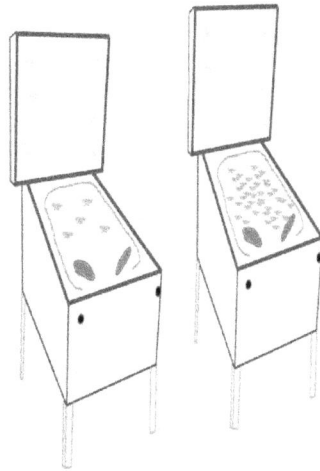

This makes us realize that our current approach to ESs has hit the wall in addressing the needs of large organizations and conglomerates. We can only make monolithic systems so big before the risk and cost to an organization are too great.

In the future, we need to break systems into smaller systems that can communicate. However, unlike the current method of creating systems where systems are created on a function-by-function basis, we instead need to be able to create systems by locality (branch, department, retail outlet, etc.) with a central architectural design focused on integration. We then integrate the systems to exchange data between localities and roll data up from all localities to a central entity for reporting. As architects, we know it is possible to create an architecture for this type of system. We just need to begin with the end in mind.

The stretch goal is to create a framework and best practices that allow us to create ESs that can easily exchange data between systems and to allow us to share functionality between systems.

I took on the challenge of developing the 3D ES architecture based on a new end that would allow us to deal with the many issues we face in delivering software to organizations cost-effectively.

I began architecting a new paradigm for enterprise software based on my experiences from actively being involved in creating enterprise software. Next, I began publishing articles and collecting feedback from industry experts. Then I successfully developed the database utilities necessary to achieve the new vision. Producing the software expanded my knowledge about the challenges and how I would have to address them.

The underlying database utilities to support the new paradigm have been developed and tested and are available for demonstration at www.3denterprisesystem.com.

The software that I have produced deals with:

- performing data conversions of systems into the new model,
- managing finances,
- tracking change history,
- managing temporal data, and
- automating master data management.

It is important to note that I do not believe that the solution is for me to create this software and then become the sole licensee of the software. The new paradigm for enterprise software simply will not work with a proprietary model. Instead, it needs to be an open-source project, where the community can extend the model as it needs to as it matures. It also provides a line in the sand to measure solutions produced by other architectures from a functionality and performance perspective.

When I wrote this book, I examined the root cause of the issues faced, formed principles to address them, and then successfully created a database framework to support it. Every step of the way, I took the time to rationalize my decisions, so everyone knew why things were architected the way they were. I tried to be detailed enough that an architect would have all the supporting information to create a 3D ES architecture in the way they chose.

When I created 3D ES, I did it with the help of others. The first person involved in the project was my co-author, Kewal Dhariwal. I approached him about my

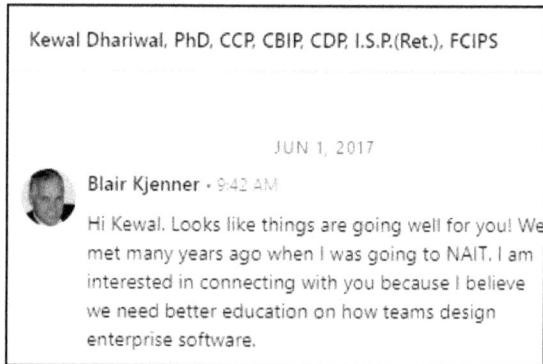

> Kewal Dhariwal, PhD, CCP, CBIP, CDP, I.S.P.(Ret.), FCIPS
>
> JUN 1, 2017
>
> Blair Kjenner · 9:42 AM
>
> Hi Kewal. Looks like things are going well for you! We met many years ago when I was going to NAIT. I am interested in connecting with you because I believe we need better education on how teams design enterprise software.

realization that there was no education offered that helped architects and developers create ESs. Kewal is a dedicated researcher and developer committed to advancing the information technology industry through education, training, and certifications for over 35 years. He has built many systems in the UK, Canada, and the US, and understands how we approach enterprise software and the issues we face. Kewal's knowledge of the business and understanding of communicating that to technical resources has been exceptionally valuable.

In 2017, Kewal immediately connected with the stretch goal I was trying to achieve and has been a tremendous supporter. To verify and support these concepts, he sought out the views of an international subject matter experts such as William (Bill) Inmon, Dr. Peter Aiken, Len Silverston, Debra Henderson, Susan Earley, Steve Hoberman, Chan Beauvais, Dr. Bradley Jensen, Don Gotterbarn, Ken Bainey, Greg Lane, Dr. David Marco, and many others from ACM, IEEE, CIPS, DAMA International and ICCP Board and Certification Committees. In addition, he sought out the views of many published authors, international companies, and CIOs for their views to validate an innovative way of approaching integration for enterprise systems development.

This book intends to fully rationalize the architecture for the 3D ES so that it is well understood and can be flexibly extended in different contexts. Another goal of this book is to provide a foundation of educational material that can be used to educate a workforce on creating such an ES for everything from a small standalone organization up to a conglomerate.

The size of the ES Market in 2022 was reported to be 669,819 million according to Gartner.[5] Certainly, with an annual expenditure of 669,819 million, there is room for investigation into a new approach to ES software, particularly if it will substantially improve our efficiency in creating ES Software and, more importantly, the efficiency of organizations that use this software. 3D ES will allow organizations to lower cost and increase their flexibility to adapt quickly to changing business conditions. It will fully leverage higher data governance, data security, data quality, data warehousing and lakehouse,[6] data analytics, machine learning, and artificial intelligence, exponentially increasing the benefits organizations get from using it.

We hope you will read this book with the same intent we wrote it—to improve our industry and help it reach a new level of productivity and effectiveness.

This is an altruistic project for Kewal and I, where we can give back to a career we have enjoyed.

---

[5] https://www.gartner.com/en/newsroom/press-releases/2021-10-20-gartner-forecasts-worldwide-it-spending-to-exceed-4-trillion-in-2022.

[6] See Appendix A and Appendix B.

1 Problem/Needs Analysis

1.1 Introduction

Throughout the book, you will see our current methods for architecting ESs referred to as the 'old paradigm' and the new methods described as the 'new paradigm'. The term *old* is not to disrespect all of the software industry's amazing accomplishments. Instead, *old* and *new* are succinct terms about what is and what can be.

This section aims to rationalize the architectural principles for the new paradigm. To formulate these principles, it is important to understand why the old paradigm for ESs is failing to allow us to create systems for large organizations and conglomerates. Specifically, with old paradigm systems, we will evaluate:

- Why do we struggle to integrate applications?
- How does this impact the organizations we serve?
- How does the IT Industry create systems?
- What is the root cause issue with our current approach?
- What are the contributing factors to the root cause issue?

1.2 Our current approach to systems

1.2.1 Why are systems so difficult to integrate?

If systems were easy to integrate, there would be no need for a new approach. The reality though is that systems are very difficult and costly to integrate, and we typically only achieve a small amount of integration between the systems we attempt to integrate.

To illustrate why systems are so difficult to integrate, we will use a scenario where a large oil and gas company has ten interrelated systems and needs to implement a contract management system. Naturally, the organization would like to integrate the contract management system with its existing systems. However, when they analyze the well-related data in the ten other systems they use, they find that each system maintains a different number of wells and different

attributes about wells. No one system has all the wells and all the attributes in one place.

This is because each system that captured data about wells was designed independently, and the architects captured whatever attributes were necessary for the business function they were automating. For example, architects would have likely captured different attributes about a well for a production accounting system than a well maintenance system. When you look at all the attributes about a well, you may find some common attributes, but they have different meanings. For example, well status appears in every system, but every system has a different number of well statuses with different meanings.

Even if we could get past the issue that every system had different attributes to describe a well, the next issue we would hit is the identifiers (primary keys) in a database used to uniquely identify a well. Each system may have its own unique identifier for the same well. If systems need to exchange data for the same well, then a central registry for all wells will need to be created, and then the IDs in each system will need to correlate those IDs to a common well identifier. Then, all the attributes for a well in each system will need to be mapped to the central registry.

Once we get past that issue, we need to know which system has the version of the well record that is going to be considered the gold standard or single source of truth for that record. It would be convenient to believe that one system could be the gold standard for all well data, but we would quickly figure out this system does not include all the other systems' attributes. Furthermore, we probably would find that some systems are better suited to be the gold standard for a given attribute than others.

As difficult as integrating well data sounds, consider that well data is just one type of data that the contract management system has in common with the other systems. Critical data such as division of interest (ownership), royalty owners, rates data (expense rates), contact data (partners), general ledger account, cost-center codes, and location schemes are just a few examples of data that would exist in a contract management system that would also exist in other systems.

This data is known as master data, and it represents the bulk of data that needs to be exchanged between systems. From my personal experience, master data (which includes reference data)[7] represents more than half the tables that exist in each system.

If you shared all master data between all the tens or hundreds of systems, the complexity of the task would be

---

[7] Reference data contains information such as who, what, and where this data is used in a business process; the permissible set of data values; and a categorization system to assure consistency across data items.

both overwhelming and cost-ineffective. As such, only small integrations between a few systems are typically performed.

To summarize, the top five reasons it is difficult to integrate applications are:

- Data structures and naming/code conventions for data are based on each development team's preferences which make it extremely difficult to map data from one system to the next.

- There is no control over how IDs (primary keys) are assigned, so the same record can have different primary keys in different systems. This makes communicating between systems for the same record difficult.

- If every system can update data about a given record, then which system has the trusted version?

- More than 50%[8] of the data that exists in a system is master data. If systems are to be truly integrated, then all forms of master data should be shared.

- The more systems an organization has, the more it will struggle with integration.

---

[8] From the authors' personal experience. Master data also includes reference data.

1.2.2 How is our approach to systems affecting organizations?

Many organizations experience significant issues with integrating their systems. The more systems an organization has, the more it will experience these issues. Also, the more related organizations that an organization needs to share data with, the more challenges it will face. The resulting loss in efficiency and effectiveness is huge from a productivity perspective. Some of the issues that organizations experience are as follows.

1.2.2.1 Inefficient administrations

Some organizations will have hundreds if not thousands of systems. The biggest challenge with having so many systems is having to manually keep all of the common data in sync. In addition, consider the impact of users accessing many different systems to perform their role. More importantly, engineers, doctors, supervisory staff, and highly trained professionals often waste their talents with data re-entry. This is a huge productivity issue faced by most large and small organizations alike.

1.2.2.2 Heavy dependency on spreadsheets

Spreadsheets have become the stopgap solution for dealing with integration issues and unsynchronized databases. If we were to compile a list of all spreadsheets that an organization needs or uses to operate, the numbers would be enormous. Even today, most of the continuing education classrooms are filled with people learning how to use spreadsheets more effectively. Spreadsheets are used like a database and often contain critical corporate data (not visible or accessible to the central systems), residing mostly on personal computers (in the workplace or at home). Consequently, they become huge security hazards, or even worse, result in lost data.

1.2.2.3 Data integrity issues can result in financial consequences

An organization with many different systems that are not integrated can have financial consequences. As you read in the introduction, I worked on a project where we recovered millions in lost revenues. This is a significant issue caused solely by systems not being integrated.

These issues not only result in missed revenues but also missed expenses, which set the organization up for a surprise liability. This problem is not new. In the 1970s, a Lloyd's of London Brokerage house had not reconciled two very large international brokerage accounts dealing with insurance premiums for over five years because of their inability to connect payments with policies. This resulted in a large tax liability due to exchange rate gains, which nearly bankrupted the organization when the accounts were updated. Straightening out mistakes between companies is expensive, often manual, highly administrative, and creates embarrassment for the organization that caused the error.

1.2.2.4   Challenges with answering simple questions

Which system is correct when an organization has many different systems that all record the same data? Each system can have its own version of the truth; typically, no one system is perfectly right.

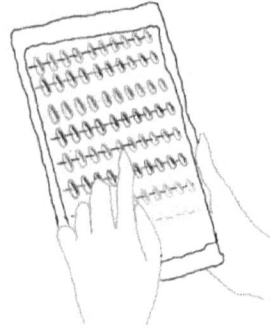

In the oil and gas scenario, mid- and large-sized companies have trouble answering a simple question such as, "How many wells do we have?"

1.2.2.5   Difficult to compile management information

For all the reasons that integration is challenging, creating data warehouses is equally challenging. If we encounter the same attribute in many systems, which system's attribute should we use? How will the data be mapped if no obvious primary key map exists? For example, with contact records, where a common primary key does not exist, it is unreliable to map based on first name, last name, birth date, and phone number. We would not be able to determine if it is the same contact in two systems, since phone numbers can be reassigned and two people with the same name can have the same birth date.

As a result of these challenges, if an organization has hundreds of systems, most of the systems will present difficulties in providing accurate data and so will not be used to populate the data warehouse.

Not only does this make management reporting complex in the face of missing data, but it also limits an organization's ability to take advantage of new technologies such as AI.

This challenge only grows when you consider that systems are continually changing, affecting every data source used for analytics and management reporting. No wonder management faces difficult choices in trusting the data and resulting analytics.

1.2.2.6 Implementing and maintaining information systems is expensive

If an organization has hundreds of systems, it has designed and created hundreds of common functionalities, which it must now maintain. For example, how often are teams (re)designing user interfaces that control how users sign onto a system, and then a security procedure in one system limits them to the functionality and data they are permitted to access? Furthermore, much effort goes into (re)designing how users will search, browse, and edit data, and drill down to child data and then construct a supporting framework.

Whether a package or a custom system, be assured that it costs you much effort on work and rework. Both approaches to software (custom development or package installation) come with their own set of challenges. The challenge with custom systems is that each system may be developed with different technology, which means the organization will need to keep fragmented support teams with experience with all the different technologies used.

Another challenge is that common functionality cannot be easily created in one system and shared with all other systems. Say your organization wants to implement the SCRAM (Salted Challenge Response Authentication Mechanism) security protocol in hundreds of its systems. It is not hard to imagine how expensive that would be and the minimal level of source code sharing between systems.

The cost to our macro economy is huge. The only saving grace for global competition is that every country's software industry is following the same erroneous practices.

1.2.2.7 Summary

Consider how costs have changed in the IT industry over the past several decades. What you will notice is we see technological improvements that drive down costs in everything but ESs. Consider the technological improvements we have seen with computer hardware. Every year the cost of more powerful computer hardware goes down. What we can get today in computing power would have cost us many thousand times more, decades ago.

The opposite is true with ESs. Years ago, a million dollars was a large budget for a system. Today, we are seeing budgets of billions of dollars and we do not blink an eye. It's just what it costs. Savvy salespeople and frustrated IT folks are bamboozled into imagining that the shiny new software package will solve their data and systems problems.

In the early days, a cost-benefit analysis was a part of the development process. Today, we have given up on that notion, which is considered a cost of doing business. When you think of a system costing billions of dollars, it is not hard to imagine why we don't bother trying to make someone believe there is a return on investment.

When you look at the collective solutions the IT industry has delivered to large organizations, involving hundreds if not thousands of systems, the costs to create and maintain those systems, and their resulting low usage, it reveals how badly we have failed as an industry in creating efficient software at a reasonable price. We need to think about why we are not seeing the same productivity gains with ESs that we are seeing in other parts of the IT industry, such as storage, servers, processors, and the Internet.

We have more powerful software development tools than ever before. So, the main culprit is our methodology for creating systems, and more powerful software development tools are helping us to create silo systems faster than ever.

1.2.3 How we create systems

When you step back and look at how we create systems, it is not hard to see that we have a problem.

Management gives teams a scope when they create a new system. Then the team analyzes the requirements and comes up with a design. During the process, they architect everything from how users sign-on, limit users to seeing only the functionalities they are permitted to, and manage contact data for users, staff, customers, partners, and suppliers. In the process, they design:

- How they are going to structure data and assign names to tables and attributes.

- How primary keys are defined on a table-by-table basis based on their preferences.

- What database engines they are going to use.

- What tools they want to use for developing the user interface (UI) based on the latest and greatest technologies.

They seldom look at the other systems in an organization and the data they will be duplicating, and rarely discuss maintaining this duplicate data. Further compounding the problem is the lack of rules for managing data integrity. This further muddies the waters when trying to determine a single source of truth for similar types of data across various systems.

They will make every effort to make the best system within the available budget. The completed system will be thrown into the mix of systems an organization uses, only to figure out it cannot be integrated to any large degree.

In the long run, the system will need to be supported. The older the system gets, the more the technology will grow out of favor, and then more the organization will struggle to find resources to support the system. Eventually, the system will need to be re-written and the cycle repeats.

When the organization cannot take the pain of architecting systems by function this way, it will eventually turn to an ES vendor to implement a large integrated system. This can be an expensive and risky project, and when it is completed, it may not eliminate nearly as many functional systems as the organization had initially hoped. Now another problem is created because the organization will be overly dependent on the ES vendor with little ability or desire to switch to a different ES vendor.

In addition, the organization will find that the more they customize the ES, the more challenges they will have with upgrades. They will also find that it will not be easy to reshape the ES to meet new needs.

However, it should be kept in mind that at least the ES vendor can get a system in place and that it is better than attempting to deal with systems on a business function by business function basis (if the cost to implement the ES was reasonable).

Why are ES vendor teams more successful than the organization's development teams at creating systems that last?

It is how the ES vendor approaches the problem. Whether an IT team creates a custom system, or an ES vendor extends their system to include a new module, the process starts much the same way. The teams are given a scope and list of requirements that need to be automated. Where it differs for the two teams is what architects can and cannot do. First, the ES vendor team is given strict parameters to operate within. Their developers are not given choices such as:

- What primary key mechanism do they want to use?

- What naming conventions for tables and columns they want to use?

- What technologies do they want to use?

Also, the developers do not redesign and develop common functionalities that exist in every business system.

Instead, ES vendors educate their developers on how to extend their platform in a standardized way to meet the unique needs of any business. This maximizes their efficiency and allows them to create functionality shared across systems.

The ES vendors fall short because their architectures are not designed to share all forms of data between all the systems they deploy. For instance, imagine if we could implement ESs in all entities involved in healthcare. Each ES would fully automate the entire business of each healthcare entity and meet its unique needs. Now imagine that we can deliver services in one entity and then pass the details of those services to another entity along with the financial details. Or imagine we could take detailed data from each healthcare entity and roll it up to a central entity for analysis, reporting, and ML/AI.

This is not possible in today's ESs for the following reasons:

- Today ESs do not use any special protocols for primary keys. In fact, many use a combination of composite keys and incremented integers. This makes it difficult to exchange data between systems and roll data up from many different systems for reporting.

- They have no way of sharing master data between all the systems and then broadcasting updates when it changes. At best, you may see they will have a central data store for shared master data. This implies that one entity controls all the master data but actually master data can be contributed by any business entity and some master data only applies to them.

- They have no way of identifying who owns a record. For example, in our healthcare scenario, if every system can update patient data, then which patient record in which system represents the correct version?

Would a proprietary model work for the industry even if an ES vendor could perform these functions? For example, if SAP produced a solution that allowed its customers to easily exchange all forms of data, would all organizations have to switch to SAP if they wanted to exchange data? It would be like the internet being owned by a single business or blockchain being owned by a single business.

The reality is we cannot have one ES vendor that controls the whole market for ESs, and the likelihood of all ESs working together to create a solution for exchanging all forms of data is low.

1.2.4 Root cause of our issues

There is a common pattern in how we construct systems, whether it is a custom system, Software as a Service (SaaS), software package, or ES system.

Teams are given a list of business functions to automate. Then they design a system to accommodate them, including a unique user interface and a database unlike anything previously created. Then they attempt to integrate it with all the other uniquely designed systems, only to find out they cannot do so to any large degree, which ends up creating large challenges for the business. This forces us to create monolithic systems, which can only get so big before the implementation projects become unmanageable. In summary, the root cause of our issues is that we have set the bar too low for what is actually required by businesses. All of our model

curricula, educational programs, and workplace expertise focuses around creating silo systems when we really need education around creating integrated ES that can meet all of the financial, administrative, and operational needs of a given business entity and are capable of rolling up and exchanging data between business entities in a secure fashion.

The IT Industry has become experts at creating silo systems.

1.2.5 Key issues

This section discusses some key issues that stem from the root cause.

1.2.5.1 No overarching principles

There is no common, comprehensive strategy in our approach to designing systems that would allow all of the systems created to communicate and share data easily and functionality between systems. Let's compare our approach to creating systems to another profession like accounting. Here is what it would look like:

Imagine if there were no Generally Accepted Accounting Principles (GAAP) for accountants. If that were the case, there would be no common terms such as debit, credit, income statement, or balance sheet. Instead, each accountant would devise their own unique method for tracking finances for organizations. Imagine the duplication of effort and how difficult it would be to compare finances from one organization to the next. Trying to implement Sarbanes Oxley (SOX) or Canadian SOX (CSOX) would be impossible and fraudulent, and misleading financial information would be common, making investor risks intolerable.

In fact, seemingly every profession has evolved to develop principles and standards that have helped them to accelerate. This applies to teachers, engineers, lawyers, physicians, and any other profession.

The IT Industry has had no such development of principles and standards. Is it because we got off on the wrong foot and took a proprietary model? What if other professions had adopted a proprietary model? Where would they be today?

The IT Industry is in desperate need of principles and standards for how it creates ESs for organizations.

We need to step back and develop a new approach to ESs designed from the bottom up to mobilize data between systems. This will help us take large complex systems and break them into smaller ones that can communicate. It will also empower us to easily move data between related organizations.

As a result, the IT profession will be capable of developing ESs for organizations that allow them to enter data once and then share within the organization and with its customers and suppliers.

1.2.5.2 Minimal education for creating ESs

At the core of every business is a financial administrative system. Yet when you look at education for developers in technical colleges and universities, there are currently no programs that educate developers on how to create these types of systems and then extend them to meet the unique needs of organizations. Likewise, no architecture courses in technical colleges educate an architect on how to create fully integrated systems across the organization.

As such, developers and architects create silo systems one at a time with disparate databases and then attempt to integrate them. This has led to a scenario where teams decide everything about how systems are created, from the technologies used to the naming conventions in databases to the appearance of the user interfaces.

1.2.5.3 Difficult to cleanse enterprise data

If data is the new oil, then why are we architecting systems the way we do with each system having a disparate database with little or no possibility of exchanging data between systems or aggregating data from all systems?

The old paradigm is more like 'data is the new dirty oil'. In the new paradigm, we need to recognize the value of data right from the beginning of system development so we can easily exchange data between systems and roll up data from all systems to a central repository for reporting.

1.2.5.4 New approach is required for a new end in mind
'Best of breed' has been a cherished approach over the years. The idea is to pick the best system to automate a particular business function and then integrate it with the other systems. Examples of these systems are an accounting system, a contract management system, a work ticketing system, etc. The flaw with this approach is that old paradigm systems are developed in silos and integrating them to any large degree is challenging.

The 'best of breed' approach provides short-term gains for long-term pain.

As a profession, we need to step back and look at what is important to our customers and align our approach with that. If the goal is to fully integrate data within an organization and then to be able to exchange data with partners, suppliers, and customers, then we need a new approach to architecting systems designed with the end in mind.

1.3   What solutions have we tried to address the problem

In the past, many solutions have been proposed to deal with our problematic issues with enterprise systems. This section discusses these solutions and how they fail to address the problem.

1.3.1   Software as a Service (SaaS)

Some organizations believe the answer to their integration problems is purchasing SaaS solutions implemented in the cloud. The idea is to just select best of breed SaaS providers from the web and then all your data will be in the cloud ready to integrate. However, the opposite is true. When systems get implemented in the cloud, organizations often lose access to the databases that support the system. In these cases, an organization may be limited to data extracts provided by the vendor.

> *Moving from locally hosted solutions to SaaS hosted in the cloud has made it more difficult for organizations to integrate their systems.*

This increases the challenges of pulling data from all the SaaS systems implemented in the cloud and aggregating them in the data warehouse. It also makes it difficult to integrate SaaS applications produced by different vendors.

1.3.2   Electronic Data Interchange (EDI)

Some organizations implement sophisticated EDI solutions. These tools allow one system to publish data that another system imports. Certainly, the tools help with integration, but there are still challenges:

- Each system has a different number of attributes for the same record.

- Each system has its own primary key to identify data.

- One system will unlikely contain all the attributes necessary to populate all the other systems.

- Every system can update a record, so there will be many different versions of the same record.

- Companies do not effectively manage the integrity of the data.

The EDI tools are just a "Band-Aid" when integrating all data from all systems.

1.3.3   Powerful software development tools

IT professionals are often guilty of looking for the next software development tool to be the silver bullet to solve our problems. Instead, what happens is that what is state of the art today becomes dated two years from now, which causes teams to jump from one technology to the next for every new system created.

Definitely, we have seen development teams increase their performance, but that only results in more silo systems getting created faster. For example, if we implement a more powerful software development tool and still create systems with disparate databases, we are still going to struggle with integration.

Large organizations end up with many disparate systems over the years, each requiring a dedicated support team. This results in challenges for the organization to support these systems. The increasing maintenance costs eventually force them to re-write perfectly good systems because they can no longer find resources to sustain them.

1.3.4   Data warehouses

Data warehouses are our best tool for viewing all organizational data in one place. The challenge comes when an organization has hundreds or thousands of systems that contain data that needs to reside in the data warehouse. As good as data warehouses are, they are only as good as the data we send them. Furthermore, they do not solve the root issue, which centers around how we create systems. The reality is we cannot design systems in silos and then expect that we can easily pull the data together in a data warehouse and solve our data integration problems.

All the challenges we face in integrating systems also apply when trying to pull data from disparate sources to integrate in a data warehouse. To reiterate, these challenges are:

- Each system has its own identifier for the same data, which makes it difficult to connect data across systems.

- Different types of databases are involved.

- Many sources of truth. Which one do you believe?

- Systems change, which results in changes to the data warehouse.

1.3.5 Artificial Intelligence (AI)

The dream is AI will play a significant role in the future for organizations. However, the reality is that for AI to be truly successful, an organization must have a clean set of data that touches all functional areas of the organization.

The challenge that data scientists face with AI is that most of the effort goes into aggregating data from disparate sources that were never designed to work together. This limits how much real AI work they can accomplish. The reality is that most organizations have many different databases designed in silos and cannot be integrated to any large degree for the purposes of AI.

1.3.6 Methodologies

Some enterprise architecture methodologies (e.g., TOGAF) help organizations architect large and complex enterprise systems. These methodologies are certainly important, but how organizations implement them still results in siloed systems. For example, if we used independent teams, all certified in the same methodology, and they were given the same requirements, we would see all of the same issues we see now. Each system would have a unique user interface and a unique database. If we tried to integrate the systems, all the same issues we discussed would exist.

The methodologies are important but the focus on a micro perspective of addressing enterprise needs of a given organization rather than a macro perspective of creating enterprise systems for organizations that have an inherent capability to exchange data with other organizations.

1.3.7 Master Data Management (MDM)

MDM is a discipline that involves procedures for controlling master data across all systems to improve data integrity and allow data to be connected across systems.

The challenge with master data is that it is multi-dimensional and needs to be shared by business entities within an organization and sometimes with its partners, customers, and suppliers.

The highest-level entities need to be able to create master data, and then lower-level entities must be able to inherit and augment this data. Sometimes, the levels of sharing go down many levels. This is a difficult requirement for MDM to accommodate on its own.

Certainly, MDM is a step in the right direction, but all the integration challenges still apply. It is not uncommon for large organizations to have tens, hundreds, or even thousands of systems. Even the most disciplined organizations will face challenges trying to keep master data in all systems synchronized.

1.3.8 Universal data models

There are books that identify models for all types of data that organizations commonly use. Universal data models are an important part of the solution, but we need to go further than that if we address the larger data integration issues.

For example, if all organizations created their systems based on universal models, we would still struggle to exchange data between systems because of issues with primary keys. Each system defines its own primary key for the same data, so how do you map records from one system to the next? How do you record governance since which system's version of the record do you trust? Also with data transfer, if we had to enhance each system to be able to exchange data, it would represent a tremendous duplication of effort.

1.3.9 Microservices architecture

A microservices architecture is gaining popularity by architects to solve issues we are facing with creating monolithic applications. It promises to allow us to create fully integrated, scalable, and maintainable applications. It will also address deployment issues because instead of deploying all microservices with every deployment, the team only has to deploy the ones that changed.

The microservice architecture is based on the premise that each microservice is self-contained and that developers can link microservices together to achieve complex functions.

Each microservice maintains all the data it needs to accomplish its purpose. Developers design the data structures that a microservice requires and then decide where to store the data. The data can be stored in a common database or developers can choose the storage location on a case-by-case basis.

Microservices typically work with NoSQL databases that are not ACID-compliant. The definition of ACID compliance is as follows:

- Atomic – the database either does all the updates involved in a transaction or none of them.

- Consistent – the database forces committed data to comply with defined integrity rules.

- Isolated – the database ensures one transaction does not impact another by having one transaction fully complete its work before the next one starts.

- Durable – the database has built-in logging features that allow it to recover from a server failure. If a transaction is committed, the transaction will be restored properly when the server is restarted.

ESs require ACID-compliant databases because they deal with financial data tied to other administrative data like rates and terms for agreements.

Even an organization like Netflix, one of the leading microservices advocates for their website, recognizes they need an ACID-compliant database for their financial and administrative data.[9]

If microservices are used with a database that is not ACID-compliant, then all the requirements that ACID compliance accommodates must now be handled by

---

[9]   https://netflixtechblog.com/netflix-billing-migration-to-aws-part-iii-7d94ab9d1f59.

developers on a case-by-case basis. For example, to maintain atomicity, developers must create code to be able to roll back a canceled transaction. This creates additional coding work, and as much as developers try, they can never fully accomplish ACID compliance like a database.

For example, if a developer created code in their microservice to roll back a transaction, data integrity will be compromised if the database server fails partway through the rollback process. This creates an unacceptable risk.

The next consideration for a microservices architecture is that it does not deal with the issues that prevent us from easily moving data between systems like using standardized data structures, using special primary keys to transfer data between systems easily, or using record governance so we always know where the gold version of a record resides.

This is not to say that the microservices architecture has not had success. They are well embraced by developers for many types of applications, especially when they do not require ACID compliance.

1.3.10 Open-source ES solutions

A simple Google search will reveal a multitude of open-source ES solutions. Some will allow you to download all source code for the application easily. Certainly, open-source ES solutions are a major component of the ultimate solution. Having said that, we will be no further ahead unless the open-source solutions are designed and built from the ground up to address the issues we are experiencing with old paradigm solutions. Namely, these systems will need to use a new mechanism for primary keys so that a primary key for a record can be created in one system and then transferred to any other system without ever having to change it. The systems will need to have record governance built in so we always know the book of record. The systems will need to have features built-in for sharing master data between systems and change history capabilities built in so we can detect when records change.

These features go right to the core of how the systems are created and retrofitting them after the fact would likely result in a system rewrite. Having said that, there are excellent lessons to be learned about how they deploy and manage an open-source solution.

1.3.11 Summary

IT experts are anxious to solve the problems we are experiencing with how we currently create systems. There are lessons to be learned from each solution discussed in this section. For example, the ultimate solution will have a data warehouse and data lakehouse component,[10] leverage MDM practices, be an open-source solution, and leverage something similar to universal data models.[11]

These disciplines mentioned in this section will tie together into a holistic solution designed from the ground up to allow organizations to exchange data between systems easily.

---

[10] William (Bill) Inmon, from Data Warehouse to Data Lakehouse.

[11] Len Silverston, Universal Data Models, LLC.

2 Defining the Stretch Goal and Vision

2.1 Introduction

Large and small companies have made gallant efforts to address the myriad of integration issues that we are experiencing today. Still, as an industry, we are falling far short of providing mature standards and principles. This section further describes our stretch goal to provide new standards and principles for enterprise systems for the industry by beginning with the end in mind. The stretch goal and vision were defined using the following process:

- Define the critical success factors.

- Define the stretch goal.

- Define the objectives necessary to achieve the stretch goal.

- Define a high-level vision of how the new paradigm will work.

2.2 Critical success factors

If we are going to come up with a new approach to creating systems, then there are some critical success factors we must abide by:

- Allow all solution providers to find a place in the new paradigm to contribute. This includes hardware vendors, database vendors, software vendors, and system integrators. This also includes individual professionals such as architects, business analysts, and data architects.

- Provide backward compatibility for old paradigm systems to connect into the new paradigm.

- Allow organizations to take back control of their systems instead of being bound to a single vendor with little ability to move to a different vendor.

- Allow organizations to address their unique needs.

- Dramatically improve the cost efficiency of creating and supporting systems.

- Allow architects and developers to create software which is shared among organizational systems.

2.3 Stretch goal

Organizations have long set stretch goals for themselves that have helped them to achieve far more than they believed possible. For example, Japan had a stretch goal of having trains that went at 120 miles per hour to transform the country. Jack Walsh leveraged stretch goals for General Electric (GE) and set a goal of a 70% reduction in defects. In both cases, at the outset, no one believed that it was possible, but they focused all of their efforts on accomplishing it so they could reach their goals. The IT industry desperately needs a stretch goal for creating ESs. As such, the stretch goal for the new paradigm is as follows:

To create ESs based on a standard template and best practices that are capable of easily exchanging data in a secure manner with other systems and allow us to share functionality between systems.

In the end, we want to see the same cost benefits with 3D ESs that we see with computer hardware. With computer hardware, our cost of computing power (processing speed, memory, data storage) continually declines. There is no reason we should not be able to accomplish the same thing with ESs.

2.4 Objectives

The key objectives that are necessary to accomplish the stretch goal are as follows:

1. To create best practices and standards around how enterprise databases are designed. We need to understand the data that is at the core of all business systems and then standardize best practices for database design to efficiently store, retrieve, and process increasing volumes of data in an integrated manner.

2. To change the way we uniquely identify data, so that we can move data between systems without changing identifiers. We need to put more thought into how data is identified so that when we assign identifiers for records, they live with the record no matter where it goes.

3. To implement controls so that we always know which organization/locality holds the book of record for a given entry. If every organization can update every record, then we don't know which organization has the true version of data that we can

trust. We need controls in place, so that it is evident where the book of record for a given entry exists.

4. To parameterize the automation of business functions so it is less tied to technology. Business applications are all too often rewritten because they are developed with tools that have gone out of favor which makes them difficult to support. In the new paradigm, we must allow business analysts and developers to parameterize the definition of ESs so the underlying framework can have technology upgrades without causing the ES to be re-developed.

5. To eliminate duplication of effort that exists around creating and maintaining application frameworks. Application frameworks are being recreated for almost every system that gets developed. It is a tremendous duplication of effort. In the new paradigm, we need to understand what is common about enterprise application frameworks and then have organizations specialize in creating application frameworks that follow the same protocols. It is exactly like how we approach web browsers. We have web browsers produced by different companies that are capable of presenting web pages consistently. Instead of the application frameworks reading HTML, like web browsers do, they will read application automation definitions that are produced with similar consistency. This will speed up software

production, reduce errors introduced by programmers, reduce costs, and assure applications are built on time.

6. To educate and certify a workforce capable of deploying interconnected ESs. This is very much like what the Chartered Professional Accountant (CPA) designation has done. It has defined a body of knowledge, educated and certified individuals and organizations to provide the services based on the body of knowledge, conducted reviews to ensure practices were being followed, and continually educated their members on following the practices. By doing so, they have elevated the status and compensation for all CPA professionals. The same type of designation is required for ES professionals. ES professionals need to be educated and certified based on standardized principles. They need to be monitored to ensure they are following the practices and being continually educated. By doing so, ES professionals will gain respect, elevating their status and compensation. ICCP,[12] an international and respected society of professional associations in computing, is one organization ready to provide a low-cost, central certification standard in ES for all business, data, and computing societies.

---

[12] https://iccp.org.

2.5   Vision for the 3D ES

The vision for the new paradigm is similar to how the internet works. The internet has evolved to the point that it has become interconnected with the world. At the center is a non-proprietary core that allows all parties to contribute and to be able to address their unique needs.

We propose the same vision for 3D ESs. It is a non-proprietary core with an inherent capability to communicate and can be extended and customized to meet the unique needs of any organization.

3D ESs will be created based on a new core ES with an inherent capability to exchange data securely. IT professionals will be educated on how to extend these systems to meet the organization's unique needs and be able to transfer any kind of data between systems.

> *3D ESs will transform how an organization communicates with its suppliers, customers, and partners. Data can originate with a supplier and flow from one organization to the next along the supply chain to the final consumer.*

Large organizations can break its systems into smaller systems that can communicate with each other. Often these systems will be divided up based on business units or sub-business units within the organization. With large organizations, data will flow between 3D ESs subsystems to a primary 3D ES.

Interconnected organizations like healthcare will be able to implement 3D ESs for each healthcare provider's organization and integrate them so that common master data can be shared among all systems and transactional data can be rolled up to the highest levels for reporting.

Governments can break their systems into many small 3D ES fully integrated subsystems. You will see systems such as citizen registries, land registries, and vehicle registries interconnect, and functional systems such as healthcare and education systems connecting with those registry systems.

Each system will have core functionality for managing contacts, finances, assets, activities, and human resources, but can be extended to meet the unique needs of any organization. SaaS vendors can extend on core structures to perform specific business functions that will connect to any core 3D ES.

Software development will become even more structured, where it will become more consistent and production oriented, rather than remaining a craft industry where application developers create disparate systems using the technology of the day. Continuous systems improvement will be enhanced significantly since a global set of contributors will be able to add value to the open-source 3D ES core systems.

The 3D ES approach is an alternative model to privately controlled ES applications, yet at the same time will allow ESs to interact and interface with it. So, instead of organizations fully relying on ES vendors, they will have their own development teams experienced in extending the core systems to suit their unique needs.

Our focus on creating systems will flip the axis from focusing on creating systems by business function to creating systems by locality. In the old paradigm, we create systems based on business functions we need to automate, and once it is done, we throw it into the mix of applications. For example, if we needed an asset maintenance system, organizations would either buy or custom-build one.

In the new paradigm, we will focus on implementing systems by locality. A locality will have all the functionality necessary to perform its role. So, if one or more localities required an asset maintenance system, then a 3D ES component would be created, and then each localities system would be extended to include it.

As time goes on and the open-source base of software increases, teams will either be able to buy or build components to meet their specific business needs.

2.6 Summary

One of the biggest challenges with the old paradigm is trying to merge data from different systems for reporting. As previously mentioned, 80% of the effort related to ML/AI is dedicated to merging and cleansing datasets. In the new paradigm, merging and cleansing datasets is done automatically in a utility that can take data from many different 3d ES databases and automatically aggregating them into a data warehouse. It will merge data that is common to all systems and maintain all foreign key references. Not only will it do this, but it can also update the data warehouse when any of the feeder databases change.

In the new paradigm, a utility that is capable of generating a data warehouse based on systems that make up a conglomerate has been developed and tested. This utility is available for demonstration at www.3denterprisesystem.com.

In the old paradigm, a utility like this is impossible to create because databases are as unique as fingerprints and the old paradigm is not designed from the ground up to exchange data. Even ES vendors cannot create a utility like this because their systems are not developed with the principles on the new paradigm. The vision of the new paradigm is to fully achieve the hypothetical project described at the beginning of the book.

The new paradigm will transform how business will be conducted. Data will be entered once and used many times within and outside an organization. Organizations will be able to roll-up data from many different systems and truly engage the power of ML/AI.

The new paradigm, as difficult as it may appear to accomplish, is considerably easier than what we do currently. In the old paradigm, we recreate the same functionality repeatedly using whatever technologies and design standards the development team chooses. We then spend endless hours trying to integrate and aggregate data from all the disparate systems, only to figure out it is too costly. As a result, we force users to key data from one system to the next and then use spreadsheets to reconcile. The old paradigm is far more difficult and labor intensive than we care to recognize.

With the new paradigm, we will work smarter by using an approach designed from the bottom up to achieve our desired end state.

When considering competition between countries, some countries will be forced to sit back and wait for their architects and developers to get on board with the new paradigm. These countries will be slow to adopt it because too many of its architects and developers will still be chasing the next silver bullet technology.

Other countries will cautiously review the 3D ES approach, but once they understand its value and how it will speed up the organizations for global competitiveness, there will be large-scale buy-in, and they will support it with education, funding, and legislation. These countries will rapidly evolve to create an integrated network of 3D ESs that can share functionality and precise data between systems.

The same applies to large companies and conglomerates that either choose to hold on to the old way of creating systems compared to large companies that recognize the limitations of the old paradigm and make the change to transform their IT systems into 3D ESs.

Certainly, a paradigm shift for ES development is going to occur. We simply cannot keep creating systems the way we do. There is too much pressure to aggregate and share data between systems.

As soon as a few systems are created with the new paradigm, the light will begin to turn on for organizations and then eventually the detractors.

In summary, we will never be able to fully achieve our aspirations for what we all know is possible for business systems until we step back and transform to a new approach that begins with the end in mind.[13]

---

[13] Franklin Covey.

3   3D ES – Design Principles

3.1   Five key principles

3.1.1   Introduction

Just like the Generally Accepted Accounting Principles (GAAP), there needs to be a strict set of principles that is adhered to if we are going to accomplish our overall goal of creating systems designed from the bottom up to exchange data. In our industry, we can accomplish them in two ways: Generally Accepted Application Development Principles (GAADP) and Generally Accepted Data Management Principles (GADMP). This section discusses each of those core principles.

3.1.2   Core data models

3.1.2.1   Introduction
Core data models encompass the common data that you see in any organization. They include subjects such as

contacts, finances, activities, assets, and contracts, among others. The models are built based on a 'less is more' philosophy where the attributes represent those commonly encountered for a given subject. For example, consider the attributes for a contact. If we look at most systems, name (elements of a name can vary by country), gender, and birth date are the most common attributes to describe a person. This was true 20 years ago and it is true today. The same applies to financial data. Every financial system, at its core, are journal entries. Journal entries have common attributes such as the chart of accounts number, cost center number, transaction ID, amount, and description. If you compiled data dictionaries across all types of organizations from all types of industries and then entities and attributes that occurred in most systems, you would find the core entities and attributes that make up the core data models for 3D ES.

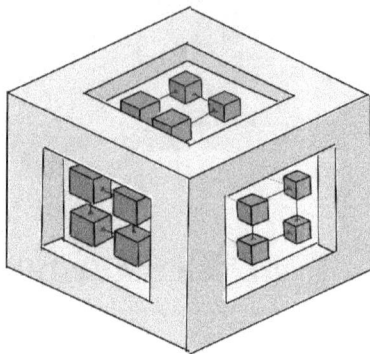

3D ES connects all the core data into a fully integrated model that connects all the core data (e.g., contacts, finances, activities, assets, and

contracts) This model is designed to be extended to meet the unique needs of any organization.

When you think about an ES vendor that strives to meet disparate industries' needs, it uses core models. It has models for managing common types of data, which do not change from one organization to the next. For example, an ES vendor does not develop a new way to manage financial transactions when it implements its system with a new industry. Instead, the vendor expands its core models to meet any business's unique needs.

3.1.2.2 Tiers of a data model

There are three tiers to a new paradigm data model. At the center of the data model is the core model. It represents the common data that you would see in almost every organization. Core models are produced based on analyzing models for all organizations and then identifying the common entities and attributes.

The next tier is the industry model.

An industry model builds on the core model to represent the unique needs of an industry.

Industry models are produced in the same way. They are produced by identifying the commonly encountered entities and attributes that exist in industry systems. It is produced based on the same "less is more philosophy" from the core model. If an organization deals with multiple industries, it will have multiple models represented in the industry model. The industry model for an organization only contains the entities of interest. For example, an oil and gas service company would only have selected entities from the oil and gas industry model. The last tier is the custom layer. This layer allows an organization to extend the core and industry models to meet the unique needs of an organization. The image above depicts the three tiers for a given organization. The center of the model is the core model, middle tier is the industry model and the outer tier is the custom model.

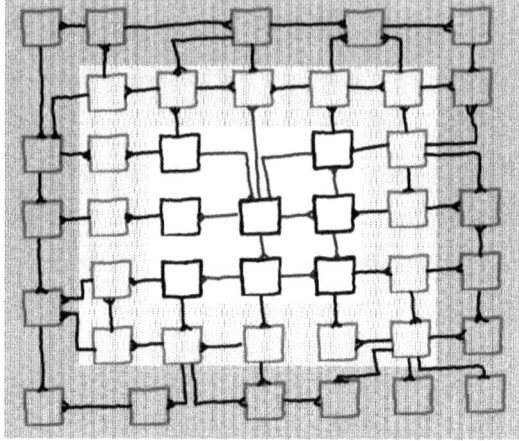

3.1.2.3 Temporal

The core models have built-in features for managing temporal data. Temporal data is data that is time-sensitive. One example of temporal data is payroll data. Payroll data describes how a staff member will be compensated. These details come into effect and then can change when a staff member is promoted. The core model neatly organizes temporal data according to its effective date.

There is a considerable amount of data that is classified as temporal data within ES's. Having features for temporal built into the core models, helps us to manage this data efficiently.

3.1.2.4 Change History

The core models also have features for managing change history. Change history is an audit log of changes to data. Change history tracks who made the change, the date and time the change was made and the command/menu option that was used. It also tracks a before and after image of all the records that changed, as a result of the change event. Change history tracks changes to both temporal and non-temporal data.

3.1.2.5 Core Model Data

The Core Models not only contains core data structures, but it also contains core data. For example, reference tables like GL Transaction Status or Address Type are prepopulated with values. Organizations can inherit the data in the core model and then augment it to meet their specific needs.

3.1.2.6 Benefits of core models

Core models have many benefits for creating systems in the new paradigm:

- We can refactor industry models to integrate them with the core models and use consistent structural patterns and naming conventions.

- They will allow organizations from different industries to exchange data based on the common types of data we see.

- They allow us to create common functionality (most notably financial utilities, change history utilities, and master data exchange utilities) that we can use as a template for other types of utilities.

- They will help architects get a head start on architecting data for an organization by allowing them to focus on what is unique about that organization.

- They reduce the risk of creating new ESs because architects are utilizing core models and related source code that has been tried and tested.

- We can expand them to meet unique business needs. For example, the model can take a core data about financial transactions and extend it to track any type of financial transaction.

3.1.2.7 Summary

Core models support the data dimension of 3D ES systems. The data models are organized in a way that core data, industry data and data unique to a business entity can all be supported. The temporal and change history features of core models support the time dimension of the 3D Model. These features allow us to see how data changes over time.

Using core models is not a new concept. ES vendors have always used their core models to create applications for organizations with disparate mandates.

If we are going to be successful in the new paradigm, then we need to develop 3D ESs using core models that manage the data common to all organizations regardless of their mandate. Then, we need to extend the models using existing industry models, such as models for the oil and gas industry, manufacturing, transportation, retail, and government.

Core models are one of the cornerstones for sharing common data among organizations regardless of their mandate.

3.1.3   Primary keys

3.1.3.1   Introduction

This section deals with primary keys. A primary key is a value or combination of unique values that uniquely identify a record. For example, a customer is assigned a unique primary key. The primary key for the

customer is recorded on all records that relate to that customer. For example, if there are activities performed for a customer, then the primary key of the customer will be recorded as a column on the activity record. This column is known as a foreign key. If we need to retrieve all data for a customer, we can select all activities where the foreign key recorded on the activity is equal to the customer's primary key.

3.1.3.2 Types of primary keys in the old paradigm

The three most popular types of primary keys are incremented integer, composite keys, and Universally Unique Identifier (UUID).

Here we explore the weaknesses of current primary key designs before introducing the new 3D primary key requirements and architectural design pattern below

---

An incremented integer key requires the system to assign the next available number. For example, for GL account number, if the last ID assigned was 101, when the next record is created, it would use 102.

A composite key comprises as many values as needed to uniquely identify a record. For a GL account, a composite key could be all the components of an account number that make up the GL account number.

A UUID is also known as a Globally Unique Identifier (GUID) in Microsoft technologies. This ID is generated from a random number and may include information components like time stamps and MAC addresses. The premise of this ID is that if a large enough number is randomly generated, it can be used as a primary key and used in any other data set without colliding and corrupting the data record.

The pros and cons of each of the different types of primary keys are discussed below.

3.1.3.2.1 Incremented integer

Primary keys impact how the data gets stored. With incremented integer, most databases will store the data neatly in the order the data was created. This creates advantages for how efficiently the system uses disk space and speeds up retrieval. This is particularly important when joining data from many different tables into a single view.

Incremented integer is one of the more popular choices for primary keys because they are small and can accommodate many unique values. For example, a 4-byte integer can accommodate almost 4.3 billion unique values. The size of the key results in excellent performance in indexes. Users and developers can easily refer to an incremented integer. For example, in our GL account example, the primary key could be 102, which is a nice short-hand value for referencing a particular GL account.

The challenge with incremented integers comes when you attempt to merge data from two different systems. For example, these issues may occur if you took all records for a table in one system and copied it into the same table in another system:

- Duplicate records with the same data but different IDs, depending on which system created the ID. For example, if two systems created the same GL account, it would likely have a different account number in each system.

- Primary key collisions in that the same ID may have been used in both systems.

For these reasons, it makes it unworkable to try to move data from one system to the next without spending copious efforts to deal with the primary key issues. It also is the reason that it is so difficult to merge data from many different systems into a data warehouse.

3.1.3.2.2   Composite key

Composite keys are another popular choice for primary keys. The large ES vendors use composite keys extensively. Composite keys are simple to understand and implement, but in the context of the new paradigm have the following issues:

- Composite keys have an issue when data that was used as a primary key changes. For example, when a GL account code is used as a primary key, it creates issues if the structure of the GL account code needs to change due to the organization expanding or changing mandates.

- Composite keys cannot be used for all tables because not all tables have natural primary keys that make each record unique. A contact record is the best example of that. You cannot reliably combine first name, last name, birthdate, and other contact attributes to uniquely identify the contact. In this case, you must use a different type of primary key. As a result, composite keys will be used for some tables and other primary key methods for others, resulting in a mixture of primary key methods.

- Composite keys make it difficult to create common utilities because one or more columns can identify every table. For example, creating a central change history mechanism is difficult when the primary keys change on a table-by-table basis.

- Composite keys can be bulky when recorded as foreign keys on child records. For example, a composite key can be tens of bytes long compared to an integer key that is four bytes long. This increases the size of foreign key indexes, resulting in performance impacts for retrieval.

3.1.3.2.3   Universally Unique Identifiers (UUID)

You will need a really big number when generating a random number and then throwing it into the mix with other random numbers based on the premise that it will never be the same as a previously generated number. This works with old paradigm systems because they operate in isolation within minimal exchange between systems. In the new paradigm, we will blend records of hundreds or even thousands of systems in one place. If we used UUIDs on every record in every system and started combining data from an increasing number of systems, the chance of creating duplicate IDs will increase, and at some stage, record collisions will corrupt the data.

Even without collisions, there are some other inherent flaws with using UUIDs on every table everywhere to identify records uniquely:

- **UUIDs are bulky.** A UUID is 16 bytes, four times the size of a four-byte incremented integer ID. This bloats the data storage necessary to store primary and foreign keys. The bigger issue, though, is retrieval performance using indexes. The computer reads a block of data to locate a record in an index. A big performance issue is that the computer can only retrieve one-quarter of the data in an index read compared to a four-byte incremented integer key.

- **UUIDs are not user-friendly.** For instance, if a user wants to know the ID assigned to a contact record, it takes a string of 32 bytes to communicate it to them. It also means developers cannot reference UUIDs without copying/pasting them.

- **UUIDs cause data storage problems.** When we create a new record, most databases will place the data in the database based on the primary key's value. With UUIDs, it means the data gets randomly spread out. This inflates the storage, leaving lots of empty spaces, resulting in bloating. There are also performance issues when trying to read records randomly dispersed. This creates such a big issue that developers will create an additional incremented integer column on tables that use UUIDs and designate that as the primary key, just to get around the storage issue. This works for a single system but causes problems when you try to merge data from two different systems.

Given all the weaknesses with the design and use of current primary key mechanisms, we need a significantly better primary key design to resolve these problems.

3.1.3.3   Requirements for the new 3D primary key

Here is a summary of the requirements for the new primary key.

- **Mechanism must be the same for all tables.** If we are going to have any chance of moving to a 3D ES, then we need a consistent method of creating and managing 3D primary keys. That means it will not work if we have incremented integers on some tables, UUIDs on others, and composite keys on the remaining tables.

- **Must be as small as possible.** Size matters when it comes to 3D primary keys. The bigger the key, the more it will impact data storage and read performance. As such, the key needs to be as small as possible.

- **Must allow for data to be stored efficiently.** As previously mentioned, UUIDs don't work because it causes data to be randomly dispersed, which causes bloating and read performance issues. So instead, the 3D primary key must be somewhat sequential to store data efficiently, which will speed up data retrieval and reduce bloating.

- **Must be unique across all systems.** The goal is to define a 3D primary key when creating a record and never change the 3D primary key for that record no matter where the record travels. We must design the key for portability and mobility across systems locally and internationally.

- **Must be expandable to grow as our use of our systems grow**. Just as IP addresses have grown from IPv4 to IPv6, we need to allow the IDs to grow to meet new needs.

- **Must be quickly generated for bulk inserts**. When we insert massive amounts of data, we need the database to assign 3D primary keys quickly when the record is stored. An example of such a process is generating large amounts of journal entries for an annual billing process. This requirement forces us to have high-performance algorithms for generating 3D primary keys, so we do not impact performance.

3.1.3.4   Components of the new 3D primary key

The 3D primary key for the new paradigm addresses these requirements. It has two components:

1. **System ID**. The System ID component identifies the system that generated the ID. When creating a new 3D ES, a utility will be available that copies down the Core 3D ES to a local database. Embedded in that database is the System ID that is assigned.

2. **Record ID**. The Record ID uniquely identifies the record within the system for a given table. It is

created using built-in features for incremented integers so that no two records will be assigned the same ID. For example, if we created a journal entry for System 123 and the last journal entry created for System 123 was 1000, then the next journal entry would be created with a System ID of 123 and a Record ID of 1001.

3.1.3.5 Size of the key

In the future, the 3D primary key will be a binary format with a variable length so that it can increase in size as required. The initial size of the key will be an eight-byte integer value. The initial format of the key will support 1.8M systems and one quadrillion Record IDs.

3.1.3.6 Know which system created a record

The 3D primary key includes information that identifies which system created the record. This is critical information used for the next principle, which is record governance. One of the key principles of record governance is that if a system creates a record, it automatically governs this record. The opposite is also true. If a record is imported into a system and the System ID does not match the local System ID, then the system will not have governance over the record.

When record governance is transferred from one system to the next, we create governance records in both systems because it represents an exception to our rule for System

IDs. Record governance is discussed in more detail in the next section.

3.1.3.7   3D primary keys are a cornerstone of the framework

It cannot be overstated how important it is to design the right 3D primary key for this purpose. Doing this right at the beginning of architecting any system is especially important. If you do not get it right, then everything else in the architecture will be harder, if not impossible, to organize and manage.

For instance, creating a change history capability that ties to the user interface and tracks changes on a transactional basis would be impossible to do cost-effectively if we chose to use composite keys.

Another example is being able to exchange master data between systems with no programming. It would be difficult to do so if the 3D primary key was not designed for this purpose.

3.1.3.8   3D primary key example

This section shows how 3D primary keys and foreign keys look when data is merged together from multiple systems.

Below are two different tables that have been rolled up to a main system. Each system is assigned a different system ID. The main system will be 1000 and the subsidiary systems will be 1001-1003.

Activity Data for System 1000

ID	Description	Performed for	Performed by
1000-1	Provided telephone support	*ABC Co* *(1000-3)*	*Ann Lee* *(1000-1)*
1000-2	Sales call	RBY Co. (1000-4)	Sheila Lowe (1000-2)
1001-1	Performance review	Dan Smith (1001-1)	Bill Adams (1001-2)
1001-2	Develop software	NBD Co. (1001-3)	Dan Smith (1001-1)
1002-1	Attend training course	MKN Co. (1002-12)	Wendy Li (1002-1)
1003-1	Attend meeting	ABC Co (1000-3)	Jim Snow (1003-7)

Contact Data for System 1000

ID	Name
1000-1	Ann Lee
1000-2	Sheila Lowe
1000-3	ABC Co.
1000-4	RBY Co.
1001-1	Dan Smith
1001-2	Bill Adams
1001-3	NBD Co.
1002-1	Wendy Li
1002-12	MKN Co.
1003-7	Jim Snow

In the above tables, the key points to observe are as follows:

- The first portion of any ID is the system ID which identifies the system that created it.

- When a new record gets created, the record ID component is automatically incremented to the next available number. For example, if we created a new activity record in System 1000 it would be assigned the ID 1000-3.

- We have the option of merging all records or just records of interest. For example, in the contact registry we have only record 1002-1 and 1002-12 for system 1002 and no other records.

3.1.3.9 Assigned System IDs

When architects create a new system or systems for an organization, they will map out how many systems are required. When they begin the process of developing the systems, they will call a utility that automatically downloads a core utility and assigns a system id. This process ensures that no two systems ever get the same system id. The system ids are baked into the database that is created in multiple forms. The same protocols that are used for securing TCP/IP addresses will be applied to system IDs.

3.1.3.10 Summary

3D primary keys support the system dimension of the 3D architecture. It does this by allowing data to be assigned a primary key that never changes, no matter what system it is transferred to. This is critically important for being able to merge data from many different systems into a single repository for reporting. The key points about 3D primary keys are:

- None of the existing types of primary keys will meet the needs of the new paradigm.

- The 3D primary key needs to be able to exchange data between systems.

- The 3D primary key needs to be efficient from a data storage and retrieval perspective. It also needs to be efficient when generating large amounts of data.

- The new 3D primary key design has two parts. The first part is the System ID which identifies the system that created the record. The second part is the Record ID which uniquely identifies the record.

- The first version of the 3D primary key can support 1.8M systems and one quadrillion Record IDs.

3.1.4 Record governance

3.1.4.1 Introduction

The next principle in the new paradigm is the design of a record governance model. Record governance is necessary because if every system can update every record, then there is no single version of the record we can rely on to be correct. Record governance will allow us to easily manage updates to the record, by both the governor and trusted subscribers, ensuring a consistent version of the record among all the systems.

3.1.4.2   Rules for record governance

Record governance begins with the creation of a record. The system that creates a record automatically governs that record. The opposite is also true. When a system imports a master record created by another system into its database, it will not govern it by default.

Therefore, it is critical to store the System ID that created a record as a part of the 3D primary key. A system can transfer its governance to another system if required. For example, if an organization sells its interest in an asset, it transfers record governance to the new owner.

Likewise, in a regional membership system, if a member moves to a different region, then governance to maintain name and address data would transfer to the new region, and the old region would have the option of becoming a subscriber for updates to the member record.

The system will keep track of a system losing governance as an exception. The exception tells us that although the System ID portion of the 3D primary key for our record belongs to the system, the system does not have governance over the record. The exception will also tell us which other system *does* have governance of the record. Likewise, a system can use an exception to track that it has governance for a record whose System ID portion of the 3D primary key did not originate in that system.

The ability to transfer record governance only applies to master data. It does not apply to transactional data. For example, if an oil and gas service company captured activities about servicing an oil well, it would not be handled through governance transfer when it transfers those records to the oil and gas company. Instead, a custom function would be created to export the data from the service company and import it into the oil and gas company system.

Record governance for a table of data can be hierarchical. For example, the oil and gas industry could define, inherit, and extend a standardized GL account structure, which can then be adopted and extended by a given oil and gas company. In this case, we could make changes at any level, propagating down to the lower levels.

The data organization in the database impacts record governance. A governor of a record will be responsible for keeping all attributes on a record up to date. This will impact how we design records.

Record governance does not preclude subscribers from updating their version of the data. When they make an update to a record they do not govern, they will be issued a warning. If they proceed anyway, the record will be flagged as an altered one. If the governing system sends an updated version of the record, the import mechanism will compare the current record to the updated record from the governor. If they are identical, the import will proceed normally. Otherwise, the subscriber will be warned of the difference. At that point, the subscriber can look at the differences between the records and decide how to merge them.

This is necessary when a subscriber needs to update a record instantly. For example, suppose a patient has passed away in a hospital system. Even though the hospital does not govern the patient's record, it still needs to update the patient's status so that other workflow processes can proceed. This update can be communicated to the central patient registry if the hospital is a trusted subscriber.

Trusted subscribers can automatically communicate updates back to the governor. In the previous example, the hospital is the trusted subscriber. The update made to the patient's record would be automatically communicated back to the governor of the patient registry. The governor could review the change before applying it to the registry. The change history log would note that the originating change came from the hospital.

Record governance applies to groupings of records. A record group is a logical grouping of records. For example, the record group could include a contact and its address. When a system governs the contact, they automatically govern any addresses associated with the contact. In the example of an oil and gas well record, when a system governs a well record, it automatically governs the child and potentially grandchild records of that well record.

Utility functionality will be available for transferring governance that will address most organizations' needs. In addition, we can always create custom code to accommodate more complex business requirements for transferring governance. For example, in the oil and gas industry, if an organization ceases to exist and it holds governance over records, a global governance transfer will need to be done when a different organization takes over its wells. A specialized governance transfer functions would be created to satisfy this requirement.

3.1.4.3   Summary

Record governance supports the system dimension of 3D ESs. It helps us to know which system holds the gold version of a given record. This is critical when we are aggregating data from many different systems.

Record governance helps us easily manage a record's updates and have a consistent version of that record. The rules that apply to record governance are:

- The system that created a record will govern it.

- A system that imports a record from another system will not automatically govern the record.

- Record governance can be transferred from one system to another.

- Subscribers can update records they do not govern, customizing them to their context, but will be issued a warning.

- Trusted subscribers can update records that will be automatically communicated back to the governor.

- Record governance applies to groupings of records.

- There will be generic features for transferring governance, but we can supplement these with custom features for more complex business needs.

3.1.5 Transference of data

3.1.5.1 Introduction

The next principle for the new paradigm is data transfer. Data transfer states that 3D ESs must have the inherent capability to transfer data. There are several types of data exchange.

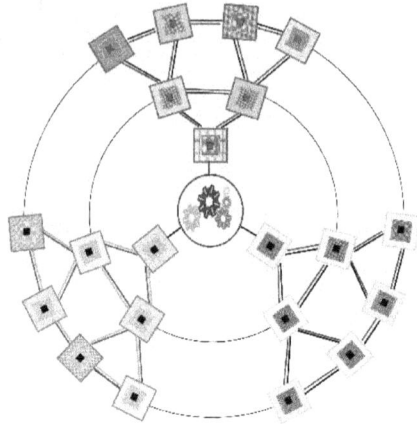

3.1.5.2 Automated data exchange

Automated data transfer starts when one system subscribes to another system's record or record grouping. When this happens, the governor system will broadcast the data to the subscriber system. Any time a record (or record grouping) is updated, the governor will broadcast the updates to any subscribers that have an interest in the record.

There are many detailed control features and considerations for automated data transfer, which we will cover later in the book. However, the high-level considerations are:

- Data transfer must allow for the scenario where the governor or subscriber has modified the table structures or associated rules. For example, if the governor required an additional column on some data it was governing, then it could add that column to the table. When a subscriber receives new updates, if it had not made allowances for the new column, it would be ignored until the system was updated to accept the column.

- Data transfer must allow for subscriptions of both temporal (time-sensitive) and non-temporal data.

- Data transfer must allow one or more column redactions for a subscription. Redacting a column involves masking it, substituting it with a new value, or nulling it out.

- Data transfer must be triggered when a record or record grouping is updated. This applies to both temporal and non-temporal data. A record grouping is a group of records that are logically related. For example, a record grouping for a contract could include the contract header record and subsidiary records for terms and contract participants.

- When a system is importing data, it needs to be able to preview changes to the record (i.e., a before and after image of all values that changed) so users are aware of the impact.

- When users are browsing data in their system, records should be highlighted if there are pending updates related to them. For example, if the governor of a record made an update, the subscriber could see the pending updates when browsing for records in the same table.

- Data transfer needs to allow subscribers to be organized into groups to minimize effort and reduce the complexity of the subscription process. For example, suppose there is an organization that has regional outlets. When a new regional outlet is created, it would be put in the regional outlet group and would automatically inherit all data to which the regional outlet group has subscribed.

- Data transfer mechanisms are primarily intended for master data. We transfer transactional data via a different process. For example, we could exchange transactional data between a service provider and its customer using a process created by the customer.

- When we import data into a system, we must catch all data integrity violations (e.g., foreign key integrity, null constraints, and unique indexes). Then, the user can either make the appropriate update so it can be processed or ignore the update and store comments on why it was ignored.

- Importing data can be set up to be automatic (automatically makes the update when the import is received and does not have any integrity violations) or manual (user reviews and approves each update that is available from a subscriber). Whether automatic or manual will depend on rules based on the sending system and the data sent.

- Importing data can trigger workflow processes. For example, if a government department subscribed to a contact in the citizen registry and that citizen moved, it could trigger related workflow processes in the department's system.

3.1.5.3 Data transfer between systems

In the core data model section, we covered the core data model tier. The core data tier representing data common to all organizations is at the center of the data model. The middle tier contains entities for one or more industries that an organization interacts with. The outer tier is the custom tier which represents the custom entities needed to address the unique needs of a business entity

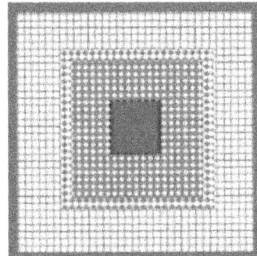

A conglomerate will have a system for each of its business entities which is illustrated by a hierarchy of connected boxes on the right. Each business entity will have a system

with a core model and industry model that is common across all business entities. The outer tier of each business entity's data model is in place to support its unique needs. The business entity systems are organized in a hierarchical fashion that goes down as many levels as required.

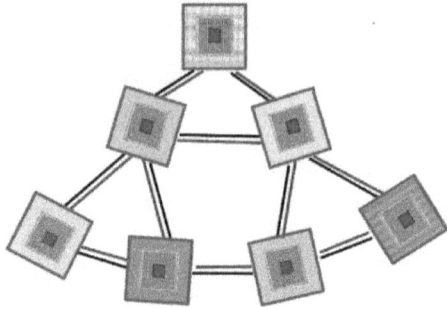

Master data is typically defined from a top-down perspective. Each level can build on master data created at a higher level. For example, GL Account codes can be defined at the highest level and then inherited by the next level and expanded upon. The lowest level can also inherit data from the middle level and expanded upon at the lowest level.

All data including transaction and master data can be rolled up from the lowest level to the highest for reporting. Also, any business unit can share data based on the core and industry tier of the model with any other.

A conglomerate can host all its data within its own servers so data can be securely shared between business units. This organization of systems is known as a subnet within the data transfer system.

The next level of sharing is between conglomerate systems. The diagram below depicts how data gets shared between conglomerate entities.

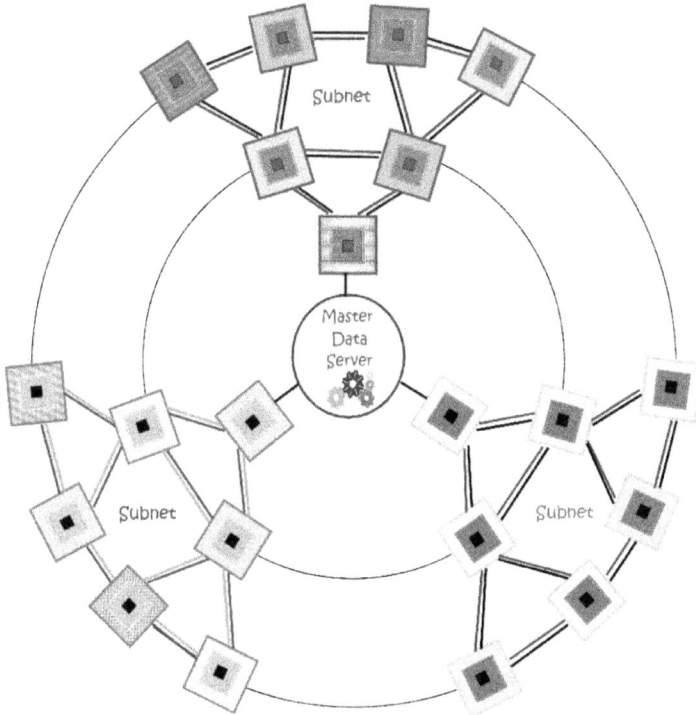

Conglomerates can communicate based on core or industry data they have in common. When a system within a conglomerate publishes data to be shared with systems outside its subnet, the data is posted on a master data server. This server operates very much like an email server. Subnets will check the master data server from time to time to see if any data needs to be distributed to systems on its subnet.

The two large circles in the diagram show how systems within a subnet can communicate directly if they need to share data directly. An example of one subnet communicating with another is an Oil and Gas service company supplying transaction and related activity data to an Oil and Gas company it is providing services to.

3.1.5.4   Data exchange using QR codes

Data can be manually exchanged between systems using QR codes (or equivalent technology). QR codes can be printed on all appropriate documents and contain the core data for that record.

The QR code will include three components: Dictionary Table ID, Row ID, and Header Data.

The Dictionary Table ID and Row ID work together to uniquely identify a record within any table for any system. For example, 0-200/2997-100, tells us it is an asset record with an id of 2997-100. We know it is an asset record because 0-200 identifies an asset table within the core model data dictionary. Furthermore, we can tell this asset was created by system 2997. Another example is 1000-100/2999-1200. 1000-100 tells us it was created by the oil and gas industry (assuming the Oil and Gas Industry model was assigned system number 1000) and that it is a well (1000-100). 2999-1200 tells us the well was first created in System 2999 and that the well has an ID of 2999-1200.

With just the 3D Primary key for a Dictionary Table and 3D Primary Key for a row of data, we can uniquely identify any type of data, for any row within any system.

The last component of the QR Code is header data for the entity. Header data is identified in the data dictionary for every entity. It represents the descriptive information that identifies the entity. For example, with a well, it would include the Unique Well Identifier descriptor. For a contract, it would be a description of the contract.

The QR Code would be used as follows. If an oil and gas service company is performing work on an oil and gas well, their staff could use an app that scans a QR code on the oil and gas well. The QR code would provide the ID for the well and accompanying details. They could then record service records for the well. When they transmit the service records to the oil and gas company, it would automatically link those service records to the appropriate oil and gas well. The oil and gas company can add a QR code on any type of asset where there is a need to collect data.

Another example would be an organization distributing copies of a contract to the related parties and including a QR code on the contract. When the parties to the contract were performing services related to the contract, they could scan the QR code on the contract. This would cause the data about the services to connect to the right contract. When the service data got communicated back to the main provider, it would automatically get connected to the right contract.

In the old paradigm, no such system exists for identifying data.

3.1.5.5 One-time secure subscriptions

In some circumstances, we will need to provide a one-time secure subscription to gain rapid access to data. This need arises due to the rapid data access requirements of the healthcare industry or first responder services. For example, in the healthcare industry, healthcare providers need access to a patient's health care records to provide appropriate service. In police, fire, and rescue emergencies, the same need exists. Sometimes quick access is the difference between life and death.

However, we do not want all the detailed data copied to the subscriber system. For example, a healthcare facility may need to provide a service for a patient. The facility will need some important patient data that they do not have but exists in another system. Therefore, the facility will use an authentication method that the patient controls (such as a feature on their phone) to access the patient's records.

This method will cause the facility to get the data back in two parts. The first will be the minimal core or header data for the patient. This will be added to the facility's system so that any other data they enter for the patient can now be easily associated with that patient. The second part of the data will be a graphical image of the more specific health data requested. The graphical image would be provided on a limited-time basis so that we only expose the patient's private data for a limited time in a specific place. The graphical image prevents the copying of text into the facility's system for personal information privacy and governance reasons.

3.1.5.6   Aggregating data between systems

As a result of core data structures, 3D primary keys, record governance, and data transference, data can be rolled up from regional systems to the highest levels for analysis. This can all happen with minimal manual manipulation of the data. It can also happen in real-time, so organizational dashboards can be produced on a periodic or on-demand basis, depending on the need and level of decision-making required. Aggregating data can provide the data to machine learning and artificial intelligence applications for detailed analysis, reporting, or automated decision-making.

3.1.5.7   Summary

Data transference is a principle that 3D ESs must have as an inherent capability to exchange data between systems.

This starts with the exchange of master data. As a result of common master data, metadata, reference data, and robust data security embedded in the new paradigm, we can exchange transactional data in an efficient, secure, and controlled manner. We can also roll up master and transactional data from low-level systems to the highest level in an organization for real-time dashboards, management reporting (dashboards & scorecards), machine learning, and AI-driven decision making. Data transference is a critical component for the system dimension of the 3D architecture. It ensures that all systems are referencing the same master data, which is critical for aggregating data across the system dimension.

3.1.6 Application framework

3.1.6.1 Introduction
In the context of this document, an application framework is a software library that contains tools for creating a user interface that simplify the development of ESs. For example, an application framework may allow a developer to create an edit form merely by specifying a collection of parameters (and business rule scripts).

The more sophisticated the application framework, the more the system can be created just by specifying system parameters.

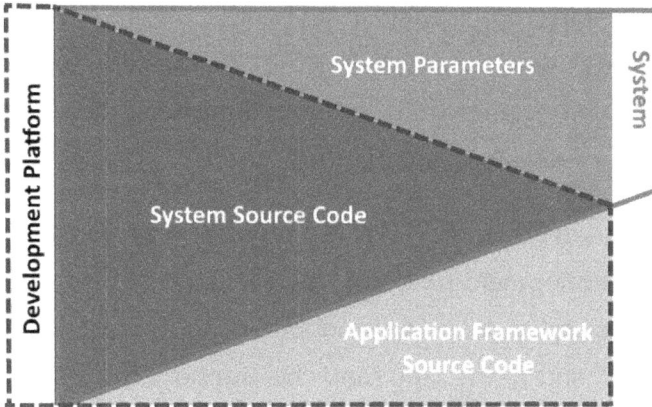

When a project team commences a system, they will create an application framework. Each team decides how much they want to invest in an application framework. How much they invest will depend on the project's budget and the development team's experience.

A system is produced using the application framework. The system can be made up of varying degrees of system source code or system parameters. The system represents the specific create forms and features that were created to meet the business requirements. Examples of such features are creating forms to add, edit, and delete a contact.

System source code is produced by developers using a development platform. System parameters are used to dynamically define forms and features. System parameters are often stored in the database. The more sophisticated the application framework, the more the system can be created by specifying system parameters. With a rudimentary application framework, there will be no capability to dynamically create the system using an application framework, so everything will need to be coded in a development platform.

The framework and system are typically created using the same development platform. A development platform can be made up of various development tools like .net, java, python, and javascript, and be supported by various database technologies.

The key challenges with a rudimentary application framework are:

- It causes the underlying system to be completely tied to the development platform. That means as the development platform ages, it can become increasingly difficult to find support resources. Eventually, an organization can be forced to recreate the system and framework even though it is working fine.

- It can result in issues with deploying changes for large systems. If a small change occurs on one form, the entire system needs to be rebuilt and re-deployed. This can represent a significant amount of effort and risk to the organization.

- It results in a system with high maintenance costs. There is no way to add a feature to the application framework and have it show up on every form. Instead, common features will need to be recreated on every form it is required.

- It can result in systems that have operating differences from one form to the next. This happens with large development teams and is due to developers re-creating common functionality in their own way on each form they are responsible for.

- It increases the budget for the system for large systems because developers need to produce more system source code to achieve the same function.

On the other hand, if the project team creates the most robust application possible, the system can be fully parameterized and have almost no system source code. With this type of framework, the underlying development platform can be upgraded or even changed without causing the system to be rewritten. This represents significant savings to the organization, because it is not recreating a system and drawing subject matter experts away from the business to redefine a system. It may seem unlikely that such a robust application framework could be created. However, consider a web browser. A web browser is just like an application framework and HTML for web pages are just like system parameters. A web browser can be created using a new development platform and implemented without having to recreate all web pages. At this point, we have only discussed one application framework for one system. Now imagine that every team is deciding how to build their application framework for their system. This represents an amazing duplication of effort in the IT industry.

If the IT industry has created a million systems, then it has recreated application frameworks almost as many times.

There is almost no sharing of application frameworks between systems. The duplication of effort means development teams are limited to how much they can spend on creating an application framework for a given system. As such, the industry tends to create far more rudimentary application frameworks than robust ones, particularly for custom systems.

3.1.6.2   Challenges with application frameworks in the old paradigm

The key points to note about application frameworks in the old paradigm are as follows:

- The more robust an application framework, the less the system will tie to the underlying development platform.

- Application frameworks are expensive to build but save money in the long term.

- Systems with rudimentary application frameworks are expensive to maintain and susceptible to being rewritten when the underlying development platform goes out of favor.

- Application frameworks are recreated with almost every system and represent a tremendous duplication of effort for the IT Industry for creating ESs.

3.1.6.3   Application frameworks in the new paradigm

The vision for the new paradigm is to define what is common about application frameworks and establish capabilities for parameterizing it. The parameters should be stored in core structures in the database and leverage all features that the new paradigm offers (3D primary keys, secure data transfer, and record governance). The vision is also that multiple vendors will be able to provide frameworks that can consume the standardized parameters and present new user interfaces. Each vendor's framework will provide different benefits, capabilities, and costs. The whole application framework model is similar to how we use web browsers on two key points:

1. The first similarity is that technology changes to the web browser do not require rewriting web pages. This is a major benefit for application frameworks

because we are not rewriting applications just because the underlying technology has gone out of favor.

2. The second similarity is that we have multiple internet browsers by different vendors, each with its own benefits and features yet capable of reading standardized web page parameters. In the same manner, we can have multiple application frameworks available from different vendors capable of presenting a user interface based on the business application parameters.

Even though we parameterize the frameworks, we are not going into production systems and changing the parameters. Instead, changes to system parameters along with changes to the database and source code occur in a development environment. Once we test the changes, they will be exported to a user acceptance testing environment and, eventually, to a production environment. We store the scripts that update parameters in source control with all the other related updates.

Entire modules consisting of parameters, source code, and database updates will be able to be batched and moved from one system to the next while maintaining the initial 3D primary key values for all parameter records.

This will substantially mitigate the typical deployment issues. With the new paradigm, we can make substantial changes to the system and not have to rebuild and redeploy the system. For example, a new browser form with edit functionality and supporting commands, including drill down, could be added to the system without rebuilding. Instead, a script would be created and tested in development, then moved through to the test environments, and finally to production, without rebuilding the system. We can even track change history on the script and undo it quickly if there is an issue.

Another significant benefit of the new paradigm application framework is that it fully addresses the issue with deploying monolithic systems.

In the old paradigm, application frameworks are often not sophisticated enough so the entire system is largely created with system source code. If even a small change occurs, the entire system needs to be recompiled and rebuilt. This can be time-consuming and introduces the possibility that unexpected changes will get in that cause issues. With the new paradigm, changes are accommodated with updates to the parameters that are applied using a database update script. This means only the parameters that need to get updated are actually changing.

3.1.6.4 Summary

In summary, an application framework includes software that controls the user interface. It also controls how the application communicates data to the database. The key points about application frameworks are:

- In the old paradigm, application frameworks were designed and developed with almost every system, representing a tremendous duplication of effort.

- We require a standardized application framework that operates much like a web browser in the new paradigm.

- Multiple vendors will produce application frameworks.

- A sophisticated application framework will dramatically reduce the effort needed to create new systems.

- Application frameworks will significantly increase the useful life of systems by centralizing technology changes to the application framework.

- Power users from the business will not need to know programming to build new applications focused on changing business needs.

- Application frameworks will help us to mitigate the issues we see with building and deploying the application.

3.1.7 Summary of the five principles

The stretch goal for the new paradigm is as follows:

To create a framework and best practices that allow us to create ESs that can easily exchange data between systems and to allow us to share functionality between systems.

If we are going to fully achieve all the benefits of this stretch goal, then all five principles must be in place. For example, we cannot use composite primary keys and still achieve the benefits. If we tried to do that, the complexity of the application would spiral out of control. Likewise, if we skipped the core data principle and allowed developers to redesign data structures from scratch for every system, we would not be able to establish core features for transferring data between systems that can be leveraged for all other types of data. The same applies for record governance, data transfer, and application frameworks. We will struggle to achieve the goal if we skip any of these principles.

The outcomes for the software industry are:

- The new paradigm for ES development will turn the software industry into a mass production industry with standardized practices, reliable delivery time estimates, and lower production costs. As a result, we will witness more on-time, on-budget, successful system implementations.

- 3D ES developers and architects who adopt this approach early will be in high demand.

- Organizations that transition quickly to the new paradigm will outpace their competition.

- In the long-term, there will be a reduced demand for production programmers, solving the shortage of sufficient technical resources.

- Following this new paradigm, existing ES vendors will rapidly reconsider and offer their own versions of how to create and implement an ES.

The outcomes for business users are:

- Simplified, standardized system interfaces.

- Improved access to timely data that crosses all functional boundaries resulting in fewer operational errors and better decision making.

- Improved efficiency resulting from data only having to be entered once.

- Better ability to leverage ML/AI.

- Ability to make changes to the system quicker to respond to changing business needs.

- Improved return on investment in business systems.

- 3D ESs will empower large organizations to aggregate data.

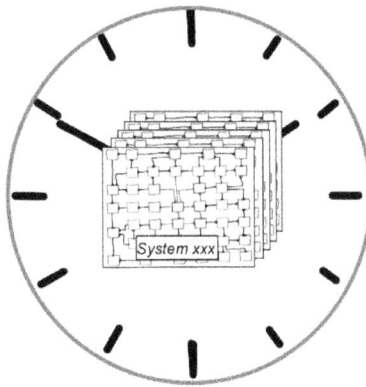

As previously mentioned, the new paradigm has three dimensions - Data, System, and Time. The diagram above depicts the three dimensions.

- The Data dimension manages data to meet the unique needs of business entities. In the diagram, it represents the outer data model box. The core model principle is the key principle to support this dimension.

- The System dimension allows us to see how the same data is shared across systems. In the diagram, each system will have its own data model and each system will have a unique number. The 3D primary key principle is the key principle to support this dimension. The data governance and data transfer principles also support this dimension.

- The Time dimension allows organizations to see how data changes over time. This is accomplished with temporal and change history tracking, which has not been discussed in detail yet. This will be discussed in sections 4.3.4 and 4.3.5.

3.2 Security

3.2.1 Introduction

This section discusses how the new paradigm system will address security requirements. It first discusses how security systems are designed and built under the existing systems development paradigm. This will help the reader understand the difference between the existing and new paradigm for data security systems.

3.2.2 How old paradigm systems address security

In old paradigm systems, architects design and develop security systems for every system that gets produced. Architects decide:

- How to secure databases.

- How to secure sensitive data within the database.

- How to protect applications against threats like SQL Injection.

- How to authenticate users and store their passwords.

- How to limit menu options and data based on a user's authority.

There is a significant effort that goes into creating security systems. However, this represents a substantial duplication of effort, considering that we do it for every system produced. In addition, a significant amount of knowledge is necessary to create a powerful security system, and not every team in the old paradigm has access to such resources.

3.2.3 How new paradigm systems address security

In the new paradigm, security protocols will be architected once for 3D ESs rather than once per system (by person/group) as we do with the old paradigm. Even if teams spend a hundred times more effort in creating a global security system for 3D ESs, it would still be considerably less effort and much more robust and universal than what we do now with old paradigm systems.

We will engage the open-source community to strengthen the 3D ES security system. One could argue that if the 3D ES security system was open-source, hackers could merely learn the vulnerabilities and break into any system. Based on that premise, blockchain should be extremely vulnerable, but it is not.

The 3D ES contains a base level of security. It uses best practices for transmitting data, storing passwords, and encryption for storing sensitive data. In addition, it controls how users authenticate (including multi-factor authentication) and how they are limited to the data and functionality they are permitted to access based on their roles.

The 3D ES tracks all of a user's activities on the system, from signing on, to accessing menus/options, to making updates. This will all be tracked in the change history module (See section 4.3.4). In addition, the 3D ES will be reviewed and certified by intrusion detection experts to ensure we address all vulnerabilities.

We have seen many failures in data and systems security. These attacks exploit vulnerabilities from these independently developed security standards by individual teams of developers.

3.2.4 Securing of personal data

Legislation is continually being developed, increasing organizations' responsibilities for securing personal data. A huge effort goes into updating systems to comply with new legislation updates in an organization with hundreds of old paradigm systems. Imagine if we could use that effort and cost to build more functions rather than on maintenance.

With 3D ESs, we can include central update features for security and protection of personal information at a core framework level that can be developed by framework providers and communicated among organizations that use their framework.

This will reduce the effort necessary to comply with legislation and reduce the time it takes for organizations to become compliant.

3.2.5 Summary

The key reason the new 3D ESs paradigm will be more secure than the old paradigm is that we can invest time and expertise in creating one security system rather than every team creating security systems on a system-by-system basis.

The 3D ES data security system will leverage the power of the open-source community to strengthen it and continually update it as new vulnerabilities are detected. As a result, organizations will benefit by not having to rearchitect and develop security systems with every system. In addition, organizations can opt to further strengthen security protocols based on their needs.

3.3 Impact of the new paradigm

The new paradigm will affect both business and IT teams. Business super-users will gain more power with IT supporting the framework-driven environment. Initially, the most significant impact will be on business units with IT located in the business unit. For instance, some business units prefer to maintain their own data even though it is common data that other departments use. There are three major areas to address in this situation:

1. **Subscriptions**. The subscription process will partially address this need, where a single department can hold governance for all records, or governance for individual records may be split across departments. The subscription process allows a subscriber department to make changes to records they do not govern to quickly deal with changing business unit requirements. It also allows for those changes to be communicated back to the governor.

2. **Common functionality**. There is a need to create functionality that benefits many business units. In the new paradigm, teams will be encouraged to create common functionality once and share it with all business units. This will initially slow down the immediate process of creating new functionality for a given business unit but speed up the process for the enterprise. As the maturity of the organization increases, this will even out the process and speed up changes for the business units.

3. **Big picture**. We need to educate and train business units to understand the big picture and reduce the temptation to seek out and implement old paradigm software solutions that may only address single business unit issues. In the short term, some exceptions may be necessary, especially if it is the right solution, but generally, the practice will require additional middleware solutions. It will be a far better and longer-term solution where teams will extend current core models or purchase new paradigm software solutions that integrate into their 3D ES.

3.4   Connecting to old paradigm systems

For the 3D ES to work, we need to smoothly migrate from old paradigm solutions to the new paradigm. This will mean we will need new paradigm solutions to connect to old systems currently existing in the organization. It will also mean that organizations using old paradigm systems will need to connect their systems to the 3D ES.

For organizations that have not adopted the new paradigm and have not implemented 3D ESs, it will need to implement a specialized 3D ES called a stub system. A stub system will have specialized capabilities for bridging between 3D ESs and existing legacy (old paradigm) systems within the organization.

A stub system bridges data from the 3D ES network to data in existing systems. This includes mapping 3D primary keys to primary keys in existing systems. It will also include algorithms for mapping data in common models to the models in the various old paradigm systems.

Developers will create interfaces between the old paradigm systems and the stub system. We can invoke these interfaces with an Application Program Interface (API) call or through direct database updates. Once we create an interface to an old paradigm system, we can share it with any other organizations that leverage the same technology.

If an old paradigm system makes an update that needs to be communicated to the 3D ES, it will call an API that will cause the stub system to be updated. If other 3D ESs subscribe to the data that is updated, the update will be broadcast to the network of 3D ESs using built-in capabilities. If the update is of interest to other old paradigm systems that an organization leverages, then updates to those systems are triggered.

Of course, not all old paradigm systems can import and export data in this manner. As a result, reports will be generated that will be referenced to manually update old paradigm systems that do not have automated interfaces. These manual processes will become automated over time.

The stub system solution will have lots of benefits for making the transition, but there will be limitations. For example, suppose an organization has hundreds or even thousands of systems. In that case, it will take considerable effort to map all the data from the old paradigm systems to the stub system.

In creating these interfaces, organizations must decide which system has the gold standard for a given record. For example, which system would it use if a large oil and gas company had tens of systems that managed records about oil and gas wells? Perhaps it would be different systems for different stages of the life of the well. For instance, in the planning phases of the well, it would export data, but another system would become the gold standard for the record in the production stages of the well.

At any rate, the 3D ES stub solution will provide great value for connecting an organization's old paradigm systems to 3D ESs. Still, it is foreseeable that the value return will be slower or not be equivalent to an organization that fully implements or transitions to the 3D ES from the outset.

3.5 Examples of 3D ESs

3.5.1 Introduction

To understand the capabilities of 3D ESs, it is important to see conceptual designs for interconnected organizations. This section describes conceptual designs for three industry examples: healthcare, oil and gas, and government.

3.5.2 Healthcare industry

Healthcare is one of the main industries to substantially benefit from integrated 3D ESs. The reason is that healthcare is a web of interconnected organizations with disparate and complex business systems that meet their specialized mandate and simultaneously have a significant need to exchange master and transactional data between the huge array of healthcare organizations. Below is an example of the complex array of data interactions, tests, and flows for one patient and one healthcare worker.

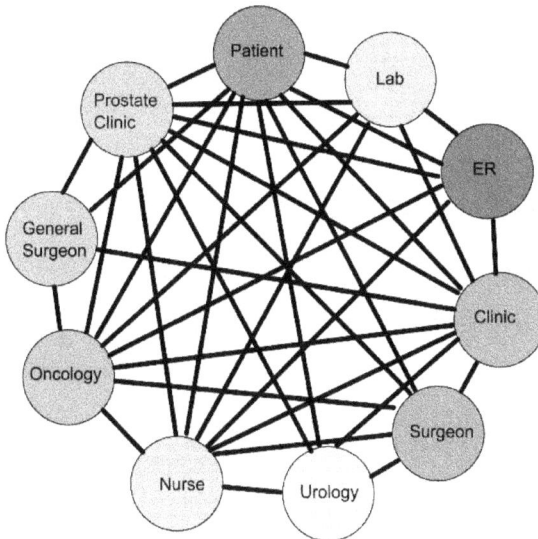

In a public healthcare system, a central healthcare body with a 3D ES will manage its business. One of the key roles of its 3D ES will be to host much of the centralized master data. The most notable will be patient data which will be an extension of data captured in the central citizen registry.

The central healthcare body will also govern all other types of master data like General Ledger (GL) accounts, treatment service types, drug types, fee structures, and many more. Master data represents more than 50% of the data in these systems, so a lot of master data will be common across various systems.

For hospitals, specialized systems will be created to address its needs. Larger hospitals will extend these systems to address their specific needs. These systems expand over time to encompass new business functions. Specialized systems will also be created for cancer clinics, labs, and physician offices. Each of these systems will manage all the business needs of these business units.

All systems will be the recipients of master data generated by other systems. For example, the lab systems will accept master data updates from both the central healthcare body and the lab organization they roll up to. The governors of the data will be responsible for maintaining subscriptions for their master data.

The healthcare provider systems will not hold detailed patient data. Instead, it will be delivered in a time-limited, graphical image of the patient data to health care providers when requested. The role of the healthcare provider determines their access. For instance, labs will see less data than emergency room physicians. If a healthcare provider does not have access to certain data due to their role, then time-limited access can be provided with a one-time subscription request.

If a patient is not in the registry for whatever reason, the healthcare provider can capture detailed data for the patient and then deliver the service and create all the required data. The patient's captured data will be communicated to the central healthcare body and used to import, create, and update the central records.

Suppose a significant change to a patient's record occurs, such as the patient passing away. In that case, we update the patient's record and send it immediately to the central healthcare body, which will review and approve the change to apply to the registry. Once updated, we broadcast this important patient data change to all subscribers.

Services delivered by a healthcare provider will be linked to the patient using their patient ID. In addition, healthcare providers will create transactional data linked to master data schemes maintained by the central healthcare body. This includes charging out services based on a fee structure maintained by the central healthcare body. The services and associated charges will be communicated to the central healthcare body. No re-keying of data will be necessary. Data will be entered once and communicated between systems.

Detailed data will be rolled up from healthcare providers to the highest level for analysis and reporting. Artificial intelligence will play a large role in delivering services. It will also automate the fraud detection and adjudication process. For example, the central healthcare body will access considerably more detail from healthcare agencies for services offered.

When you review how a healthcare system could work, it becomes very clear that for it to function in the most efficient manner possible, it needs the 3D ES. The 3D ES will allow each healthcare entity to fully meet its requirements and allow all healthcare 3D ESs to securely share critical data in a timely manner, saving lives. Furthermore, the Healthcare 3D ES network of systems will be able to communicate transactional data from service providers to the central healthcare body. This will streamline administrations, speed up payments, and increase opportunities for accessing detailed data for reporting and ML/AI.

The three dimensions of a 3D ES for the healthcare industry are as follows.

- Data Dimension – is supported by leveraging the core model and an industry model that is tailored to the healthcare industry.

- System Dimension – is supported by each system within the healthcare industry having a different system ID. As a result of 3D Primary Keys, Record Governance, and Data Transference, we are able to exchange data between healthcare entities and roll it up for reporting.

- Time Dimension – is supported by having built-in features for managing temporal data. It is further supported by a change history mechanism that tracks changes to both temporal and non-temporal data. Healthcare data has considerable amounts of temporal data related to services and the associated fee structures. It also has a significant requirement for tracking change history (audit trail) for all types of data.

3.5.3 Oil and gas industry (oil industry)

The oil industry is another industry that will greatly benefit from 3D ESs. Reasons include:

- **Partners.** A lot of partnerships are formed between companies to drill wells, transport products in pipelines, and process the products. Governments are also partners, with a commercial interest in most of these wells. If an organization is a partner in a well, then it will have an interest in having all the detailed records about the well communicated to it.

- **Suppliers.** Second, the oil companies work closely with suppliers who will provide products and services related to oil wells, such as lab testing, oil field services, and reporting. In these cases, the oil service companies collect data of interest to share between the oil companies with ownership.

- **Temporal.** Third, the data captured for oil wells is often temporal (date/time effective). Temporal data will affect how oil volumes are calculated. One example is an orifice plate size. An orifice plate has a hole in it. The larger the hole, the more that flows through it. When an orifice plate is changed to a different size, it will impact volume calculations. As such, a time-sensitive record is created whenever variables such as orifice plate size change.

The 3D ES has strong principles for managing temporal data. The change history feature is integrated with temporal, so that a detailed change history entry is created when a temporal record series changes. It identifies who made the change, the command/menu option they used, and a view before and after image of any temporal records that were affected. This is imperative to successfully manage temporal data for oil and oil-well data.

The strategy for the oil and gas industry is that oil and gas companies will recreate their systems using a template system derived from a core 3D ES. The template system will contain specialized functionality for the oil and gas industry. As a result of creating oil and gas systems based on a template system, it would enable oil and gas companies to increase the amount of data they share. This would not inhibit oil and gas companies from tailoring the models and core systems to address specific needs. Software vendors could create specialized modules that connect to standardized modules to perform specific functions. For example, a vendor may produce an asset maintenance module specifically designed for the oil and gas industry. This module would integrate with the asset, activity, contact, and financial modules.

An oil company will exchange detailed data with its partners in oil wells, starting with contract data related to the specific partnership focus. It will contain data about the oil well, including temporal updates to data, and production data. This information will also be shared with government 3D ESs. The oil well service companies will also have their own 3D ESs for managing their businesses. For example, a service company performs work related to wells under the terms of a contract. When performing the actual service work, a service worker will scan a QR code (or something similar) for a well, which will include the data entity ID, 3D primary key for the well, and header data about the well. When they perform work, the data will be captured and when it is complete, the service and financial records will be communicated to the oil company. These records will automatically connect to the right well in the well registry, the right GL accounts, cost centers, and contracts. This will be passed on to the oil well partners with a commercial interest in producing that well.

Likewise, labs will be able to capture data for oil samples. They will be able to communicate information about these samples and the related financial records to the oil company. Of course, many other types of companies provide services and products to the oil industry, and all will have their own 3D ESs and share appropriate data with their contracted oil company.

Oil companies can fully leverage machine learning and artificial intelligence because they will have increased confidence in clean, detailed, and up-to-date data to analyze. The benefits for an oil company that uses 3D ESs compared to one that doesn't will be the difference between being in business and not. If you compare a new paradigm oil company to an oil company that still has tens if not hundreds of silo systems that are not connected either to partners or suppliers, the difference in speed, agility, and efficiency will be massive. So much so, that oil companies with 3D ESs will buy companies with old paradigm systems until no companies with old paradigm systems exist.

Of course, this goal truly represents a stretch goal for the industry. The biggest challenge will be the mindset change required for the industry to kick off the process of changing how they think about ESs. The mindset will not come easily because executives rely on their technology experts. It will take time for the technology experts vested in old paradigm thinking to come around. Having said that, some oil companies will understand the limitations of the old paradigm and the possibilities of a new paradigm. It will start with a trickle of these companies and eventually lead to a flood of adopters as we begin to see success. Technology change is driving many old paradigm companies out of business. The venture capitalists will soon take advantage of the stronger and weaker companies, causing increased acquisitions and mergers in the industry. The three dimensions of a 3D ES for the oil and gas industry are as follows.

- Data Dimension – is supported by leveraging the core model and an industry model that is tailored to the oil and gas industry.

- System Dimension – is supported by each system within the oil and gas industry having a different system ID. As a result of 3D Primary Keys, Record Governance and Data Transference, we are able to exchange data between oil and gas entities and roll it up for reporting.

- Time Dimension – is supported by having built-in features for managing temporal data. It is further supported by a change history mechanism that tracks changes to both temporal and non-temporal data. This is particularly beneficial to the Oil and Gas industry.

3.5.4 Government

Most systems architects understand how beneficial it would be if government consisted of two different types of departments: registry and functional.

In the new paradigm, registry departments will manage data common to all functional departments. Examples of such registries are a citizen registry, corporate registry, land registry, road registry, and vehicle registry. In addition, there will also be administrative registry systems for managing master data common to all systems.

The functional departments will connect to the registry systems where appropriate. Examples of functional departments include education, social services, transportation, revenue, and justice.

Now that the option for 3D ESs exists, government needs can be met with an interconnected network of 3D ESs that meet the needs of individual government departments. As a result of using a network of 3D ESs, governments can begin to deal with the challenges, inefficiencies, and costs related to dealing with thousands of old paradigm silo systems.

Government 3D ESs will start from a common core connecting to the government registries. Government entities will extend these systems to meet their mandate. Large government departments will break their systems into smaller 3D ESs where it makes sense. For example, if a board/commission reports to a large government, it would likely have its own 3D ES that rolled up to the departmental 3D ES.

All the systems will be able to roll up detailed financial, administrative, and service data from the lowest to the highest levels with minimal data manipulation. For example, a government could aggregate data from all departmental 3D ESs for reporting. This will allow governments to fully leverage machine learning and artificial intelligence capabilities while providing trusted, actionable data for decision-making.

Government departments will no longer be tied to a single vendor to provide a mission-critical system. Instead, they will have the option of forming their own development teams supplemented by private sector resources where necessary. This will increase the ability of departments to make changes quickly to address rapidly changing business and political needs.

Government reorganizations, which are common, will be much easier to accommodate. We can take data from multiple 3D ESs and aggregate it in a single system or take data from a single monolithic departmental system and break it into smaller 3D ESs. It will be possible to merge two 3D ESs because of how we manage 3D primary keys and master data. Certainly, there will be work, but considerably less than what exists now when trying to merge data from two different old paradigm systems.

Fears related to the complexity of the integration task often deter many CIOs and executive directors of individual departments from implementing wholesale system changes. The question comes down to whether it is better that governments operate inefficiently with thousands of silo systems that unnecessarily consume taxpayer dollars, or should it be able to operate efficiently where data is only entered once and consumed many times?

In summary, governments will benefit significantly from 3D ESs. Governments have hundreds if not thousands of systems that they need to manage. Governments also have more requirements for custom systems than private entities because of all the unique requirements they need to address. If you look across all their systems, you will find a significant percentage of those systems capture data about citizens, corporations, and land.

3D ESs will allow data to be captured once for these entities and shared many times. It will also allow data from all government departments to roll up for reporting, artificial intelligence, and machine learning.

3D ESs will lower the costs for creating and maintaining systems by allowing functionality to be created and shared across government departments. It will also increase the useful life of systems by parameterizing enterprise applications, thereby preserving their definition and localizing technology changes to the application framework.

With this new paradigm approach to systems, we can reduce the risk and implement global policies more easily and rapidly, especially related to personal information privacy and data security. The three dimensions of a 3D ES for government are as follows:

- Data Dimension – is supported by leveraging the core model and an industry model that is tailored to the data that is shared across government entities.

- System Dimension – is supported by each system implemented within government having a different system ID. As a result of 3D Primary Keys, Record Governance and Data Transference, we are able to exchange data between government entities and roll it up for reporting.

- Time Dimension – is supported by having built-in features for managing temporal data. It is further supported by a change history mechanism that tracks changes to both temporal and non-temporal data. This is especially beneficial to government entities due to the amount of temporal data it deals with.

3.5.5 Summary

The intention of the last three examples of how the 3D ESs can accommodate the needs of interconnected business units is to expose the possibilities and opportunities. These extend to:

- Manufacturers connecting to their distribution and supply chain (like automobile manufacturers).

- Professional and social associations and unions setting up a network of 3D ESs that allow each regional system to be customized to meet its unique needs.

- International companies having systems for each country that can be customized to meet the local needs yet are able to aggregate data from all regions into a central system on a real-time basis for analysis and reporting.

The 3D ES is designed from the outset to facilitate agility and scalability, which are some of the key challenges traditional monolithic old paradigm systems face. Instead, systems will be broken into smaller systems that can be rapidly created to communicate and share data with each other in real-time.

3.6 Benefits of 3D ESs

The key benefits of 3D ESs will be as follows:

- **No duplicate data**. The new paradigm must support complete integration between all enterprise databases by recording data once and only once. This will eliminate efforts around keying, rekeying, and reconciling data. It will also simplify the production of management reports and reduce efforts around integration and the production of data warehouses, data lakehouses, or big data analysis.

- **Users have one sign-on.** In the old paradigm, users have different sign-ons for every functional system they need to interact with to perform their role. They need to learn each of these different systems' user interfaces and often use spreadsheets to collect and share data between systems. In the new paradigm, users will have one sign-on to one system with a consistent user interface for performing all business functions they need. Users will find the new paradigm offers more robust features than the myriad of applications they previously used because rather than IT building one user interface per system, it will be able to focus its efforts on creating a single, powerful user interface framework. This will free up IT resources while improving ease of access and use for business users.

- **Functionality will be developed once and shared between all types of organizations.** We develop functionality once and apply it in organizations with varying mandates. For example, we create a sales funnel system in the new paradigm. When added to an enterprise application, it will integrate with the contact registry, activity registry, and contract registry modules. Also, the menu options and forms will automatically blend into the menu system, so users will see new options for increased functionality responding to changing business needs appearing just-in-time on their menus.

- **Business-to-business communication**. In the new paradigm, all systems that follow the 3D ES protocols can exchange data securely. This includes contact, financial, asset, contract, and activity data. Central bodies, such as an accounting body, will be able to define chart of account standards, which then can be inherited and augmented by organizations. As a result, this will facilitate business-to-business communications for financial data. Organizations can switch user interfaces and the application frameworks that support them like switching web browsers. The new paradigm aims to parameterize ES applications and standardize those parameters so organizations can switch application frameworks more easily. As 3D ESs evolve, it should be possible to switch frameworks just like we switch web browsers. In addition, a complete sector of the software industry will only focus on creating application frameworks. As a result, users will witness more robust and graphical system interfaces than before and be more productive with their mobile devices.

- **Organizations can quickly adapt systems to meet their own needs.** Organizations may have to wait for a critical update with old paradigm ES package implementations. With the new paradigm, organizations will have staff members or contract resources at their disposal to extend their systems to meet their unique needs quickly. Educational institutions and professional development and training organizations will quickly fill in the need for rapid training and retraining of the workforce to satisfy the new paradigm staffing requirements. In addition, organizations will be able to purchase packages from vendors that connect to their core systems and then will be able to customize and extend these systems to meet their unique needs.

- **Security systems are more powerful and secure than ever before.** Imagine if we constructed high-level security systems into a few high-powered frameworks instead of building potentially weak models into every system created. Remember, if we are building a hundred thousand systems in the old paradigm, then we are likely constructing function-based security systems almost as often. The new paradigm eliminates this duplication of effort around security systems and, more importantly, refocuses this effort on creating a more powerful security system than in the old paradigm.

- **Management will be able to have ready access to data that crosses all functional, geographic, and time dimensions for analysis.** In today's world, management is often limited to analyzing data system-by-system because data between systems do not integrate. In the new paradigm, management will have access to data that crosses all functional boundaries of the organization. They will also be able to aggregate data from regional databases. The most important dimension will be the time dimension for analysis. The new paradigm will consistently manage temporal data (time-sensitive data) across all business systems. When you connect financial data directly to temporal data, it will exponentially improve reporting information for management.

- **Artificial intelligence will be readily available.** In the new paradigm, clean data is highly organized across the enterprise. AI engines will access functional, geographic, and time dimensions. As a result, they will be able to identify issues, opportunities, potential changes, and impacts with far greater success than organizations have ever witnessed. For this reason alone, organizations that adopt the new paradigm will quickly overtake their competitors that follow the old paradigms.

- **Return on Investment (RoI) for ESs will be a forgone conclusion**. In the new paradigm, we will eliminate much of the duplication of effort today. As a result, the cost for information technology will be driven down, and we will regain agility of IT solutions development for enterprises.

3.7 Conclusion

This concludes the first phase of this book which represents the issues with the old paradigm and identifies a new paradigm designed from the ground up to deal with those issues.

The new paradigm is based on an open-source framework designed to exchange data between systems. This framework will allow teams to create systems for large, interconnected organizations by breaking them up based on locality and then customizing local systems to meet the unique needs of each locality. Teams will understand what is common about all localities and will be able to roll that data up from the lowest levels to the highest level.

The teams will also be able to create common functionality, make it available to all localities, and customize by locality as required. We create the 3D ES methodology and application framework to support the new paradigm based on five key principles:

1. Create systems based on core models.

2. Implement a new type of 3D primary key that allows data to be assigned a unique value when created and that value never changes no matter what system the data gets sent.

3. Control which systems get to update records so that we always know which system holds the gold version of that record.

4. Provide a built-in mechanism for transferring data between systems so that a system can receive data efficiently and securely.

5. Create application frameworks similar to how web browsers and web pages work so that systems can be more parameterized and less susceptible to technology changes.

Organizations that fully subscribe to the new paradigm approach to systems will enter data once and use it many times throughout the organization. Furthermore, that data will be shareable among partners, customers, and suppliers. This will dramatically increase the efficiency of conducting business. Interconnected organizations will be able to roll data up to the highest levels for reporting and use it as a clean source of data for AI and machine learning.

The next section of the book steps into additional detail for each of the five principles. It takes each of the topics from the previous section and elaborates further. For example, although you now know the importance of core models, next, we explain what these core models look like and their design rationalization. Likewise, we cover in-depth the architectures for all major components like data exchange, change history, and others. The application framework section also maps out in detail all the key features necessary for a successful application framework.

The final section covers methodologies for creating systems based on all the book's material. It talks about all the roles that will be necessary and how existing disciplines fit, such as master data management, data governance, and enterprise architecture.

4   3D ES Architecture Design

4.1   Introduction

This section of the book discusses the design of the 3D ES architecture necessary to accomplish the principles discussed in the previous chapter. We will cover:

- Database and data dictionary
- Data exchange architecture
- Core business module architecture
- Application framework architecture

Throughout this section, we compare the old paradigm with the new paradigm. These discussions are necessary to rationalize the choices made in the new paradigm.

4.2 Database and data dictionary

4.2.1 Introduction

This section discusses topics related to the database and data dictionary. It begins by discussing the rationale related to the database engine. It then moves to a discussion about important design patterns used in designing the database and, finally, the role of the data dictionary.

4.2.2 Database engine requirements

4.2.2.1 Introduction

Databases have powerful capabilities for managing data that are imperative to a 3D ES. The most powerful of these features are:

- Maintaining integrity by:
  - o Enforcing constraints such as referential integrity, null constraints, and unique value constraints.
  - o Processing many database updates as part of a transaction and rolling back when encountering errors.
  - o Providing recoveries from server failures that occurred since the last backup.
  - o Providing backup and recovery options.

- Processing complex transactions involving many updates to many tables within a procedure.

- Extending the capabilities of the database with custom functions.

- Creating complex views that involve joins to many tables.

The 3D ES framework takes full advantage of these capabilities. A few examples include:

- Procedures to assist with automatically converting data from existing sources into a new 3D ES database.

- Routines for the financial system that provide common utilities for performing functions such as:
  o Rolling up finances for reporting based on the cost center and GL account hierarchies.
  o Performing batch approvals for transactions that are batch-oriented.
  o Exporting journal entries to an external general ledger.

- Procedures to generate change history when data is updated.

- Procedures to manage temporal data.

- Procedures to exchange master data between governor systems and subscriber systems.

- Integrity rules for referential integrity, null constraints, and unique constraints that exist within the core model.

- Error logging and the ability to control how to react to error conditions. Error logging also ties into a message table that will allow the system to be multi-lingual.

4.2.2.2   Benefits of embedding data manipulation logic

There are multiple layers within a multi-tiered architecture. Examples of layers are a presentation, application, business, and data layer. The data layer represents the database. For this discussion, we will refer to the presentation, application, and business layers as the front-end layer.

With a SQL database, it is possible to create database manipulation logic in stored procedures within the database. There are some key reasons that logic is better suited to this layer than the front-end layer:

- **Performance.** When complex transactions require many database updates, it is considerably faster to assign all the tasks to a server to perform them in one procedure compared to the application submitting the database commands one at a time.

- **Transaction processing.** It is imperative with transaction processing that either all the updates related to a transaction get processed or none of them. We cannot process any partial transactions in the database. If a layer other than the data layer is executing database commands individually, it is considerably more complex to catch errors, log them, and either rollback or commit at the end. Another issue with transaction processing is that if a process in the front-end layer begins a transaction, applies updates, and then the process is killed, it will leave database pages locked on the server.

- **Creating database commands in front-end layers is cumbersome**. There are powerful integrated development environments (IDEs) for databases that simplify the creation of database scripts. If the database scripts are created in the front-end layer, they are more cumbersome to create.

- **Updates to procedures are simpler**. Many of the updates that will need to be applied will be limited to updating scripts in the database. This is easier than deploying changes to the front-end layer.

4.2.2.3   Summary

Databases have evolved to include many features necessary for Online Transaction Processing (OLTP) systems. These features exist to provide the best performance possible while maintaining the integrity of the database.

It is impossible to skip over data integrity features just to solve other problems like scalability. Skipping data integrity is unacceptable for an OLTP system.

4.2.3 Scalability

4.2.3.1 Introduction

One of the key requirements for 3D ESs is to accommodate large volumes of data and provide access to a broad range and constantly growing number of users. First, this section discusses issues with old paradigm systems regarding this kind of scalability. Then, it discusses how new paradigm systems will address the matter.

4.2.3.2 Old paradigm design creates scalability issues

The old design paradigm is one-dimensional. It is not designed from the ground up for systems to have an inherent capability to exchange data. Consequently, if an organization requires business units to share significant amounts of data and needs to roll up data from all business units for reporting, then their only design choice is to construct one monolithic system with one database.

Not only does the single database create a bottleneck for the system, but it also means we need to segment data with row-level security so that one business entity cannot see another business entity's data. Row-level security is resource intensive and further compounds the issue of performance. For example, suppose a large international corporation requires a system for all nations, and a significant amount of master data is common to all nations. In that case, the old paradigm will force us to put it into a single monolithic database. This would cause us to implement row-level security so its organization in one nation could not see another nation's data.

All things considered, scalability quickly becomes a limitation when creating monolithic applications.

4.2.3.3   Scalability of the 3D ESs

The 3D ES approach to constructing system environments addresses the limitation of scalability by breaking away from the concept of one monolithic system by developing a network of 3D ESs.

Using the previous international company example, each nation would have its own 3D ES. Customizations to meet the unique needs of that particular nation would exist within each 3D ES. All the nation systems would be able to roll up data to the international system. There would be no need for row-level security in the systems.

If we cannot break a system up by locality, then it is still possible to take a large 3D ES, break it into smaller systems, and then synchronize data between them. In this situation, each system will have its own System ID to move data from one system to the next without 3D primary key collisions. Likewise, master data would be synchronized between the two systems.

4.2.3.4   Summary

Old paradigm systems are not scalable because it forces us to put all data within a single monolithic database. We break new paradigm systems into smaller systems that can communicate with each other, thereby alleviating this issue.

4.2.4   Database engine selection

4.2.4.1   Introduction

The 3D ES requires a SQL database for hosting 3D ESs.

This section discusses NoSQL database technologies and why they fall short. It also discusses the first database chosen to create a working model of the 3D ES framework.

4.2.4.2   Review of NoSQL database types

There are many types of NoSQL databases, including key–value pair, graph, object, and document. Some of the characteristics that NoSQL databases have in common are:

- They are schemaless. In other words, there is no predefined structure for the database. The database stores the data as hierarchical documents, objects, graphs, or key-value pairs.

- They do not force data typing.

- Typically, they are not ACID compliant.

- There is no concept of tables and joins between tables, as well as no concept of views.

- They do not support a concept of stored procedures and functions where logic is written at the database level.

The key benefit that all NoSQL databases strive for is scalability. Another reason that developers like them is because there is no schema. This means that they can make changes immediately without being encumbered to update a schema that maps out the structure and integrity rules of the database.

Developers that prefer NoSQL databases rationalize that they maintain integrity of the database in a front-end layer for the application. However, this creates several major challenges:

- Developers create code on a case-by-case basis to accomplish ACID compliance in the application where it is required. As much as they try to accomplish ACID compliance, it is not possible when you attempt to do it in a front-end layer of a multi-tiered architecture. For example, if front-end code fails part way through the process of rolling back a transaction, then the database will be left in a state of having a partially rolled back transaction.

- Developers have the freedom to maintain integrity rules any way they like. This can create inconsistencies among developers, which increases maintenance costs.

- There are performance implications with giving the database one command at a time to perform from the front-end layer instead of creating a procedure in the database and having it do all the commands within the procedure.

Many applications for NoSQL databases fit the strengths of NoSQL databases perfectly. OLTP databases are not one of them. OLTP databases need to ensure that data integrity is maintained. We cannot have financial systems that do not balance or billing systems that invoice the incorrect amount because of a data integrity issue.

4.2.4.3 One database or many

It is becoming more popular for old paradigm systems to use multiple databases. For example, a system may have a SQL database for the main data store and use a key-value database for other processes.

Having many different database technologies to implement an OLTP system creates major issues when recovering from server failures. If one database goes down or all of them do, restoring all the databases to exactly the same point can be challenging.

The rule of thumb should be if a system uses multiple databases, can the support team restore a copy of the system to another location without having to ensure backups for all databases at exactly the same time? If the answer is yes, then no problem. If the answer is no, the databases are clearly tied and recovery from server failures will be a challenge.

4.2.4.4   Required database features

At this point, we have specified that the database must be ACID compliant. Other features necessary for the database to support are the ability to:

- Support child records with many parents. This requirement creates an issue for document databases which primarily store data hierarchically.

- Create complex database utilities and functions that can perform a series of tasks within a transaction.

- Create views that join tables together efficiently.

- Natively support JSON objects.

- Support triggers.

- Support queries for recursive structures.

- Create a high-performance function to create a 3D primary key in the prescribed format.

- Support creation and execution of dynamic code.

- Support security protocols such as SCRAM.

Most but not all SQL databases can fulfill these requirements. After comprehensively evaluating several database engines for the first 3D ES framework, we chose Postgres. Although we had decades of experience with another SQL database engine and no experience with Postgres, we chose Postgres because:

- It supports over 50 data types (including JSON) and the ability to create new ones.

- It is open-source.

- It includes a search path feature that allows common database objects to be overridden for a given system. For example, if an organization needs to take one of the procedures included in the core framework and extend it to include custom features, they can do that. The framework will automatically pick up the customized version over the standard version.

- It had the best licensing costs out of the databases we evaluated at the time.

- It can manage an incremented integer for a table separate from the actual incremented integer 3D primary key.

Although Postgres is the first database we used for the 3D ES framework, it does not mean it will be the only one to use. The intention is to create the framework in Postgres and then use that as a baseline for creating functionality in other databases. The key for any other database engine chosen is that it must be capable of replicating all functionality included in the 3D ES framework. This implies that all the stored procedures and functions created in Postgres would need to be converted to a new database tool.

4.2.4.5 Summary

Choosing the right database is paramount to the success of 3D ESs. It will determine how flexible the system will be, how easy it will be to develop the framework, and how fast the application will perform.

At present, Postgres is the best database to accomplish this vision based on what the 3D ES needs to accomplish.

4.2.5 Database design patterns

4.2.5.1 Introduction

This section moves from discussing the database to discussing the data modeling patterns used for 3D ESs. These patterns give the new paradigm flexibility and power for being extended to track any organization's needs. We discuss each of the techniques in detail below.

4.2.5.2   Variable one-to-many

In a normal one-to-many relationship, a record has one parent. The parent can be any entity in the enterprise database in a variable one-to-many. Two columns are required on the child table to record this relationship. One identifies the parent table, and the other identifies the connecting row within the parent table.

This type of relationship is critical to normalizing data and making the system as flexible as possible to accommodate new situations. Below are three examples where variable one-to-many relationships are used.

4.2.5.2.1   Change history module

The change history module can track history for any table in the system. When a change occurs, a history record is generated, containing information on the change, including a before and after image of the updated record. The history record is linked to the changed record using two columns. The first column identifies the table where the change occurred, and the second column identifies the specific record in the altered table.

If we implemented this relationship with a standard foreign key relationship, foreign key references would need to be pointing to every table in the system. Not only is this cumbersome, but it also means that a database change is necessary every time a new table in the system needs to have change history tracked.

4.2.5.2.2   Activity tracking module

The activity tracking module is a generic module for tracking activities in the system. The activity module can extend to track any type of activity. Here are some examples of activities that can be tracked using the activity module:

- Billing module keeps track of what staff are being charged out on projects.

- Time reporting module for payroll determines how to pay hourly staff for their time.

- Absent time reporting module contains information about when staff were not at work.

- Call center module records interactions between staff and customers.

- Sales funnel module records sales activities between sales personnel and prospects.

- Asset maintenance module keeps track of maintenance activities performed on assets by staff.

- Land maintenance module keeps track of staff's activities to maintain land parcels.

The activity modules use variable one-to-many relationships to expand its capabilities and better organize data. For example, a staff member can not only perform activities for another contact (e.g., call center system, sales funnel system), they can also perform activities for assets with the asset maintenance module.

The variable one-to-many allows the module to centralize all activities a staff member might perform regardless of which database entity the activities might be related to. All this can be done without adding an extra foreign key to the database structure.

4.2.5.2.3   Financial module

The financial module's capabilities are greatly enhanced because of a variable one-to-many relationship. The financial module can connect a journal entry (GL entry) to any entity in the enterprise model. For example, you can connect a journal entry to a billing account, asset, project, contract, oil and gas well, or any other entity you need to fulfill a requirement.

4.2.5.2.4   Summary

Variable one-to-many relationships appear in more than ten other places in the core models. By perfecting this pattern in the core models, architects can employ it in industry models to create more flexible software that better represents the user's needs.

4.2.5.3   Subtyping

4.2.5.3.1   Introduction

When designing databases, you will often find situations where data entities have a main entity and then sub-classifications of that entity. The main entity is the supertype and the sub-classifications are subtypes. The process of modeling this data is known as subtyping.

Activity data described in the previous section uses subtyping. The main activity record contains the attributes you would encounter with any type of activity, and the subtype entities contain data specific to a particular type of activity. For example, a subtyped entity can capture data specific to asset maintenance activities in an asset maintenance system.

Contact data is another good example of data that we can subtype. Examples of contact subtypes include users, staff, contractors, vendors, customers, students, members, institutions, and associates.

Let's evaluate two techniques for storing subtype data: dynamic attributes or subtype tables.

4.2.5.3.2   Dynamic attributes

With the dynamic attribute technique, we dynamically define attributes for each supertype. For example, if we were defining attributes for various types of contacts, then we would define the attribute that applied to each type of contact. We would define the attribute's name, data type (e.g., numeric, date), and business rules for validation for each attribute. If the attribute was a foreign key that linked to another table, then all the parameters related to the foreign key table would also need to be defined.

The first challenge with dynamic attributes comes with child data only related to a subtype. For example, in a membership system with member data in dynamic attributes, all descendent data (child/grandchild) connected to member records will also need to be dynamic. This can spiral into storing a large percentage of data using dynamic methods.

Dynamic attributes also force developers to create dynamic forms for maintaining data. It also causes reporting to get complicated because the reporting engine needs to deal with attributes that reside in tables and other attributes that are dynamic. It also breaks down into change history mechanisms and automated master data management.

You could argue that dynamic attributes have the advantage of being able to add attributes on the fly. The reality, though, is we should never add attributes on the fly. Instead, we need to add them to a development environment and create scripts to move the dynamic attributes to test and production environments.

4.2.5.3.3   Subtype tables

The subtype table technique involves organizing attributes that relate to a subtype, in a separate table. For example, in a membership subtype, the common attributes for contacts appear in the contact table and we create a subtype for attributes related to members. If there was descendent data related to the member data, the descendent entity would link to the member subtype record.

Subtype tables are stored exactly in the same way as the supertype table. That means tools for working with supertype and subtype data are the same. The tools relate to creating data entry forms, writing reports, tracking change history, and transferring data between systems.

Also, we can create functionality for a supertype that a subtype can easily inherit. For example, we can create functionality for maintaining addresses and inherit that functionality for all subtypes. Likewise, we can create a capability to maintain billing accounts (receivable/payable) for the supertype and inherit that functionality for all subtypes.

4.2.5.3.4   Summary

Subtyping is an important design pattern for systems in the new paradigm. It also allows us to create supertypes and then inherit them for subtypes. As a result of using fixed tables for subtypes, we can simplify tools that process subtype data.

4.2.5.4   Recursive relationships

Recursive structures are used extensively throughout the new paradigm framework to support hierarchical structures. An example of a hierarchical structure is a fixed asset classification scheme that starts with high-level categories such as office equipment and breaks down into lower and lower categories (e.g., Office Equipment -> Computers -> Desktop).

You will likely not find recursive structures when you reverse engineer many old paradigm systems. Let's look at a GL account. Rather than using a recursive structure to represent a GL account code, old paradigm systems will often use a single column whose value is a composite of many attributes. For example, 5-12-3-123-76 is a GL account number. If you break it down, each component has an ID and description, and the entire ID represents the relationships between components. In other cases, you will also see hierarchical data get divided into a primary category table, a second category table, and even a tertiary category table.

While both these methods work, they make it harder to create common functionality. Plus, they are inflexible for users who need to reorganize hierarchies by modifying or adding new levels.

The most common reason recursive structures are avoided is because they result in complex queries. The new paradigm addresses this complexity by providing common utilities that can easily perform functions such as:

- Identifying all records that exist below a record in the hierarchy. This is useful if a user needs to select a record hierarchy and view all child data connected to any hierarchical records below the current record. With the fixed asset type example, a user drills down from a high-level category, such as computer equipment, and sees assets classified as subcategories, such as servers, laptops, and desktops.

- Identifying the lowest level records in the hierarchy. This is useful because often records will only be classified at the lowest level. For example, with a GL account hierarchy, we only want users to connect GL entries to the lowest level in the GL account hierarchy.

- Analyzing the hierarchy to identify the display sequence and level of each node. This is useful for displaying a hierarchical list and indenting each level based on its position in the hierarchy.

- Identifying relationships in the hierarchy that will cause recursive loops.

Utilities like this are possible because of the standardization that exists in the model. Once we create utilities like this and extend the core model to be used for industry models, recursive structures are often used to better represent data.

The core models even support recursive many-to-many relationships. With a recursive many-to-many relationship, a child record can have many parents. Whereas with a recursive one-to-many relationship, a child record can only have one parent.

The command/menu system is an example of a recursive many-to-many relationship. For instance, in the contact browse (search form), there is a "Related Contact Data" command that allows users to see all menu options for drilling down and viewing data about the contact. If you added a "Member-browse" command to the system, you would likely want to view "Related Contact Data" for the member. That means a command can have many child commands, but it can also have many parent commands that own it.

There are examples of queries that navigate recursive many-to-many structures for use within industry-specific models. For example, in an oil and gas system, a product flows from a well through various facilities to get to a gas plant. The product can be split up and sent to different facilities as it travels through the network and ends up at different gas plants. This relationship is perfectly suited to a recursive many-to-many relationship.

4.2.5.5 Summary

The three patterns discussed in this section are critical to creating a framework for 3D ES that is flexible enough to accommodate diverse business needs. The patterns become exceptionally powerful when they all work together. For example, the financial module uses recursive structures, subtyping, and variable one-to-many relationships. Here is how we use each of these patterns for the finance module example:

- Recursive structures can classify the chart of accounts and cost center structures.

- Subtyping can separate financial transactional data into different subtypes, such as invoices, disbursements, and cash receipts. It is also used for batches and journal entries.

- Variable one-to-many relationships can connect journal entries to any entity in the enterprise model.

These patterns allow extending the core financial system to meet any organization's needs from the largest to the smallest.

4.2.6 Data dictionary

4.2.6.1   Introduction

This section moves from discussing data model patterns to discussing the importance of a central data dictionary for 3D ESs.

4.2.6.2   Key reasons for a central data dictionary

The data dictionary provides a critical repository for recording metadata information. It describes the purpose of tables and columns. We can quickly see who references a foreign key, what forms a column populates, its default values, and constraints such as null values.

The data dictionary also contains critical information used for the following utilities.

- **Change history**. Parameters for change history appear in the data dictionary, including:

  o Parameters for which columns are checked for changes when determining whether to generate a change history event record.
  o Parameters that indicate which events (insert, update, delete) for a table cause change history event records to get generated.
  o Foreign key translations for tables to generate user-friendly versions of foreign key translations.
  o Master data exchange. Master data exchange holds information in the data dictionary about which columns are considered header columns. This is used when exporting references to foreign keys. The master data exchange module will only export header columns for the foreign key references.

- **Data conversions**. When we convert old paradigm systems into a 3D ES, we reverse engineer their databases and store their metadata in the data dictionary. Then the core models are extended to accommodate the data. The next step uses the data dictionary to create the database and generate data conversion scripts to populate it. The final step generates views and all types of constraints, such as foreign key, null, and unique constraints.

- **Used to pre-populate user interface parameters.** We can use the metadata in the dictionary to generate the parameters for many of the simple user interface forms.

- **Generate views.** This utility generates views for all tables using the business-friendly names defined in the dictionary. It will also create all the relationships to tables using foreign key references and translate the foreign key references in the view. For example, a foreign key reference to a contact will include a column that shows the contact name (based on the translation recorded in the dictionary) and the ID of the contact.

- **Generate constraints.** We programmatically generate all types of constraints, including foreign key, null, and unique value constraints.

4.2.6.3   Future for data dictionaries

The future of data dictionaries for 3D ESs is that of an open-source dictionary tool that will perform all the metadata management functions. This tool will allow metadata for 3D ES projects to be aggregated in a central repository.

This will allow the tool to use machine learning to programmatically reverse engineer systems, design new systems, and programmatically generate sophisticated data conversion scripts. This will be particularly useful when extending the core models with industry-specific models such as for oil and gas.

The tools will also accommodate attributes from custom systems it has not encountered before. For example, with machine learning, if it encounters a column called BIR_DT that is of type date on a table called person, it will interpret it as a birthdate column and will map it to the appropriate column in the core structure. It will also ensure that we follow naming conventions for tables and columns along with all other conventions, such as for primary and foreign keys.

4.2.6.4 Tools to support data dictionaries and business glossaries

Vendors of data dictionary and business glossary tools will hopefully update their products to maintain data dictionaries in a compatible format with 3D ESs. In the meantime, the 3D ES architects can use a specialized spreadsheet developed to maintain dictionaries thus far.

The spreadsheet contains all the appropriate formats and custom functions to efficiently maintain metadata for 3D

ESs. This spreadsheet will help you reverse engineer systems, create new 3D ES models and then map existing data to the new model.

The spreadsheet integrates with backend database utilities to populate the dictionary and database and then populate the database with data from existing systems.

4.2.6.5   Data model design

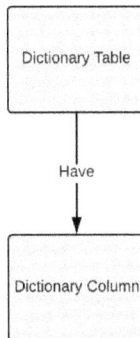

- Dictionary Table – contains a record for each table in the database

- Dictionary Column – contains a record for each column in each table in the database.

4.2.6.6   Data dictionary

Below are the elements for the data dictionary.

Table Name	Column Name	Data-Type	Purpose
DictionaryTable	ID	BigInt	3D primary key
DictionaryTable	CommandID	BigInt	Foreign key
DictionaryTable	ChangeHistoryLevel	Integer	Data
DictionaryTable	ChangeHistoryScope	Varchar	Data
DictionaryTable	Description	Varchar	Data
DictionaryTable	IsChangeHistoryUsed	Boolean	Data
DictionaryTable	IsTableTemporal	Boolean	Data
DictionaryTable	Name	Varchar	Data
DictionaryTable	NormalizedName	Varchar	Data
DictionaryTable	ObjectID	Integer	Data
DictionaryTable	PluralName	Varchar	Data
DictionaryTable	SingularName	Varchar	Data
DictionaryTable	systemModule	Varchar	Data
DictionaryTable	TableType	Varchar	Data
DictionaryTable	Translation	Varchar	Data
DictionaryTable	RowStatus	Char	System
DictionaryTable	ChangeHistoryID	BigInt	Audit
DictionaryColumn	ID	BigInt	3D primary key
DictionaryColumn	DictionaryTableID	BigInt	Foreign key
DictionaryColumn	DictionaryTableID-Foreign	BigInt	Foreign key
DictionaryColumn	ColumnSequence	Integer	Data
DictionaryColumn	DataLength	Varchar	Data
DictionaryColumn	DataType	Varchar	Data
DictionaryColumn	Decimals	Integer	Data
DictionaryColumn	DefaultValue	Varchar	Data

Table Name	Column Name	Data-Type	Purpose
DictionaryColumn	Description	Varchar	Data
DictionaryColumn	IsChangeHistoryUsed	Boolean	Data
DictionaryColumn	IsHeaderColumn	Boolean	Data
DictionaryColumn	IsEncrypted	Boolean	Data
DictionaryColumn	IsNullable	Boolean	Data
DictionaryColumn	IsIncludedInUnique-Constraint	Boolean	Data
DictionaryColumn	Label	Varchar	Data
DictionaryColumn	LongName	Varchar	Data
DictionaryColumn	Name	Varchar	Data
DictionaryColumn	Purpose	Varchar	Data
DictionaryColumn	RowStatus	Char	System
DictionaryColumn	ChangeHistoryID	BigInt	Audit

4.2.6.7 Functional components

This section discusses the functional components included with the core 3D ES.

- **Load dictionary.** This procedure accepts an export of the data dictionary from a spreadsheet. Before loading the dictionary, it checks the integrity of the data dictionary. Then, it loads the dictionary into the database.

- **Create tables.** This procedure creates the tables in the database based on the data dictionary.

- **Convert data.** This procedure converts data from existing sources into a new 3D ES database. It will deal with all types of conversion challenges, such as where a single table maps to multiple tables or multiple tables map to a single table. It will also deal with converting data from multiple systems and consolidating duplicate master data sources into a single data source.

- **Check foreign key references**. This procedure will report on bad foreign key references in the database.

- **Generate views**. This procedure will generate views in the database based on the data dictionary. It will make all the necessary joins to tables and present columns with user-friendly names. Developers can use these views as is or update them to meet specific needs.

- **Generate foreign key constraints**. This procedure generates all foreign key constraints.

- **Generate null constraints**. This procedure generates null constraints.

- **Generate unique constraints**. This procedure generates null constraints.

4.2.6.8   Summary

Data dictionaries are one of the key architectural principles that determine whether the new paradigm will succeed or fail. If an organization does not subscribe to building and generating systems based on a dictionary, it would not be possible for them to create a 3D ES. On the other hand, if the organization has fully adopted the data dictionary approach and can fully leverage an open-source tool that includes machine learning features, it would be able to rapidly convert systems into its 3D ES with low costs and be left with metadata to describe its most valuable resource – data.

4.3 Design patterns to support data exchange

4.3.1 Introduction

This section discusses the critical architectural components necessary for master data management and for exchanging data between systems.

4.3.2 3D primary key design

4.3.2.1 Overview

This section discusses the technical design for 3D primary keys. It is important to understand the research behind 3D primary key design when producing new formats for 3D primary keys in the future.

The recommended 3D primary key is a two-part key. It contains a System ID (a unique identifier for the system that created it) and a Record ID (a unique ID for the record within the table in which it was produced).

The goal of the key is to provide a high-performance 3D primary key that allows for system numbers growth while maintaining a large scope of available record IDs.

4.3.2.2   Evaluating data types for 3D primary keys
We considered three data types for primary keys:

- BIGINTs is an 8-byte integer that will store negative 9223372036854775808 to positive 9223372036854775807.

- BYTEA is a variable length datatype designed for binary data.

- BIT is a variable length datatype designed for bit data.

We ruled out UUID because it is 16 bytes long, which is too big for reasonable performance with large datasets plus it creates issues for storing data efficiently.

We completed a comparison of datatype size by creating a table with 100 million rows that only contained the 3D primary key. In the first test, we stored a value of 1 to 100M. In the second test, a max value was stored. In both cases, we evaluated the size of the table and discovered:

- BIGINTs went from 3458Mb to 6915Mb for storing 1 to 100M to storing max value. This implies that Postgres will store BIGINTs as an INT for smaller values.

- BYTEA went from 4147Mb to 8971Mb. BYTEA is variable length. As such, it uses an extra byte to record the length of the value. Another issue with BYTEA columns is sort order. If you sort by a BYTEA column rather than getting the expected hex order, you will get a character sort (e.g., 1, 10, 100 rather than 1,2,3..E, F). This will cause issues when storing data.

- BIT went from 4224Mb to 8448 MB. BIT is variable length and requires extra byte(s) to record the size of the bit column. Although BIT columns are more concise than BYTEA columns, their display is not workable.

The conclusion from the research of data types was as follows:

- The BIGINT datatype is the most effective for storing large values efficiently.

- The BIGINT datatype is the most readable.

- As we grow in the number of systems and Record ID requirements, we will need alternatives other than BIGINT. If nothing else changes, we will go to a variable length BYTEA column.

4.3.2.3   3D primary key design
The key principles of the architecture of the 3D primary key are:

- The System ID supports a maximum of 1.8M different systems. Once we use all values, we will look for a different format for the ID. We use System 0 (zero) for common values in the system tables. For example, there is a table for Transaction Status that contains the status of transactions in the financial system. In addition, default values are established that will apply to all systems. We assign default values to system 0.

- The Record ID will support a maximum of a quadrillion (i.e., 10^{15}).

- The ID will be displayed as "ss-rr" where ss is the System ID and rr is the Record ID. If the system is 0, the ID will appear as just the Record ID.

- The Record ID portion of the ID uses different ID identity ranges for different system versions. This applies to the system tables. For example, in Version 0, the Record ID starts at 0, Version 1 starts at 10,000, and Version 2 starts at 20,000. As a result of changing the identity ranges, we can insert records in system tables and move them from one version to the next without colliding on IDs. There is more about this in the version management section.

We convert the value of the BIGINT to an unsigned integer which doubles the ID values available.

4.3.2.4   Record ID will use incremented integer

SQL databases include an incremented integer feature specifically designed for performance. When multiple processes request the next available ID, this feature will ensure that each process quickly gets assigned a unique ID with minimal lock contentions.

Postgres takes this a step further and offers this feature separately from creating 3D primary keys. This is especially useful for 3D ESs because we can use a custom function that reformats the BIGINT to an unsigned number, embeds the System ID, and calls the NextVal function to get the next available incremented integer ID. The incremented integer feature works perfectly for the Record ID component because when generating records within a table for a system, we are only ever doing it for the current system. The only time we see records inserted from another system is when we import data from another system, and in those cases, the Record ID has already been assigned.

The most significant advantage of IDs with an incremented integer component is that the data is stored efficiently in the database. SQL databases work best for efficient data storage and retrieval when they are stored based on an incremented integer value. Even though a system may include data from other systems where this is not as applicable, the bulk of records a system adds will be for its own System ID.

4.3.2.5   Functional components

The core framework has the following functions available for managing IDs:

- Create ID function called to set the default value for new IDs.

- Display ID function that takes a BIGINT value and displays it in a friendly format (e.g., 1-1).

- Set Val function that resets the next available Identity Range value based on the max value Record ID encountered in a given table.

4.3.2.6   Summary

An efficient 3D primary key is paramount to the success of the new paradigm. It needs to support a System ID and Record ID and do it in a way that is efficient for storage and retrieval. The 3D primary key needs to be as small as possible to increase efficiency for indexes (i.e., a key that is 8 bytes compared to 16 bytes will be roughly twice as fast for retrieval).

If the anticipated adoption of 3D ESs is high and it is expected that we will quickly exceed 1.8M systems, then there are two options. The first option is to increase the size of the System ID from 1.8M to 18M and reduce the size of the Record ID from 10^{18} to 10^{17}. The other option is to pursue a BYTEA value.

4.3.3 Temporal design

4.3.3.1 Overview

3D ESs support three dimensions – data, time, and system. The temporal features of 3D ESs support the time dimension. This section discusses how the time dimension is supported by inherent features to manage temporal data.

4.3.3.2 Examples of temporal data

Below are four examples of temporal data.

- **Payroll data**. To pay staff, we need to keep track of the parameters related to their compensation. These parameters will change over time. For example, we assign a role to a staff member on a given date along with prescribed rules and rates for how the person gets compensated.

- **Property tax**. Property taxes are determined by the assessments for a property for a given year and based on the mill rate applicable at the time.

- **Health benefits**. A person's health benefits will be based on the plan a person was enrolled in and the benefits and limits for health benefits within that plan.

- **Oil and gas data**. Oil and gas data has a tremendous amount of temporal data. To calculate volumes for oil and gas wells, many parameters are captured based on analyzing samples of product and volume measurements such as plate orifice sizes.

4.3.3.3   Not all data is temporal

As important as it is to understand temporal data, it is also important to know what is not. Here are examples of non-temporal data:

- **Transactional data.** For example, transactions and journal entries are not temporal. We do not have a journal entry with a start date, when it is effective, and an end date when it is no longer effective.

- **Activities.** Activities in terms of who is doing what for whom is not temporal. For example, if a staff member creates an activity to indicate work that they are doing for a customer, organizations are typically not interested in seeing temporal versions of that record as it changes states. Instead, this data is captured by change history if it is of interest.

- **Fixed asset data.** Fixed asset data is not temporal in terms of what a fixed asset is, how it is classified, and its description. However, data that describes the location of a fixed asset is temporal. Over time, a fixed asset may move from one location to another.

- **Classification and reference data**. For example, we may make changes to the organization of our GL account scheme over time, but we want all data classified by that GL account scheme to be based on the current GL account scheme. We set it up this way to compare one period to the next. Likewise, reference tables like GL Transaction Status (e.g., Posted and Pending) are not temporal. For the same reason as if we add or change reference table values, we want them to be applicable for all of time.

Of course, architects can turn on temporal features for any tables they choose.

4.3.3.4   Key feature of temporal data

If a system does not have temporal capabilities, it can only maintain what the data looks like today and cannot maintain historical versions. If a system has temporal capabilities, then users can go back and update the data as of an effective date. For example, suppose a staff member's pay parameters were wrong for the previous pay period. In that case, a non-temporal system could only make the change from now on but would be unable to fix the error and re-run previous pay periods. However, in the same example, with a temporal system, the user could make the correction effective on the applicable date and then re-run the payroll batch to make all the appropriate adjustments.

4.3.3.5   Temporal resolutions

Temporal data is captured based on different time resolutions such as year, month, day, or second. For example, the resolution is a year in a property tax system. The resolution in a health benefits administration and payroll system is a day; in an oil and gas system, temporal data may be to the second.

The resolution impacts how record segments get created. For example, suppose a property tax system had a temporal resolution of a year. If any changes to an assessment for the same property occurred in a given year, there would still be only one assessment record, based on a start date and end date of no less than a year.

Temporal segments can span many periods. For example, if the assessment for a property was first set at $30,000 in the year 2000 and did not change until 2020, then there would be one segment with a start date of January 2000 and an end date of December 2020.

4.3.3.6   Old paradigm temporal data management

In the old paradigm, architects decide how to handle temporal data on a system-by-system basis, and even a table-by-table basis. As a result, you will see the following fallible designs.

- **Copying all temporal data from one temporal period to the next**. This technique involves copying all data from the current temporal period to the new temporal period each time we encounter a new temporal period. For example, the system might copy all property tax data from one period to the next in a property tax situation. This approach balloons the amount of data stored. It also creates challenges for updating a temporal record. If a temporal attribute is updated because it is incorrect, often that update needs to be carried forward for all temporal segments until a new set of temporal data occurs. This is a challenging requirement to fulfill with this old paradigm type of design. Furthermore, copying all temporal data from one period to the next may make sense when you have a temporal resolution of a year, but what happens if you have a temporal resolution of a second, as with oil and gas data? We cannot change our methods for managing temporal data because the resolution changes.

- **Keeping track of temporal changes on a column-by-column basis**. Some architects will design their temporal data so that each column in a table is held separately and has a start and end date. To view what a record looks like at any given point of time, you need to query all attributes based on a date and then assemble a record. This is an unworkable solution since the performance and complexity implications of doing this in a system with lots of high volumes of temporal data become untenable.

- **Implementation of shadow tables.** Every time a record changes, it is copied to a shadow table. If you want to see the temporal version of a record, you look at the shadow table. The challenge with this method is that it does not differentiate between corrections to temporal data (where it was wrong and needed to be updated) and actual temporal changes.

- **Event sourcing.** Event sourcing is similar to shadow tables. Each time a record changes, a change event is recorded. If we want to see a record's current state, we need to walk through each change event to see what the record looks like at any point in time. From a query and performance perspective, it would be challenging to implement event sourcing with a system containing thousands of tables and attributes. Event sourcing has its purpose in applications like workflow engines but is unsuitable for tracking temporal and change history in an ES.

4.3.3.7   New paradigm temporal data design

The new paradigm manages temporal data in a record series that contain segments. A segment represents a version of a temporal record at a given point in time. A segment will have a start date and end date when that segment is applicable. A number of segments form a record series. All segments in a record series will have the same 3D primary key. The new paradigm has utilities that enforce the following four rules:

- **Effective dates for segments cannot overlap**. There should never be two segments that overlap.

- **There should be no gaps in time for a record series**. A record series should have no gaps in time. If a temporal record does not exist for a time period, then a temporal record will still exist during that period, but it will have a row status of "deactivated". Having no gaps in our record series is to maintain referential integrity.

- **A segment can be inactive at a point in time**. Segments are set up from the beginning of time to the end of time. If a segment doesn't exist until a particular point in time, then an initial segment will be created and set to a "deactivated" status, and then that segment will get started on its actual first date of existence. If a record series is deactivated as of the most current date, then the last segment in the series will exist but be deactivated.

- **Adjoining segments should never be identical**. If the only difference between two adjoining segments is the start and end date, then we should merge the two segments into one. A built-in utility will enforce this rule. It will evaluate all segments and merge any that are duplicates.

4.3.3.8   Querying temporal data

If you wanted to list all records in a temporal table, you would query the data relative to a date (e.g., start date <= query date and end date >= query date) where the record's status was active. If joining from a child record to a parent record where the parent record was temporal, you would join where a segment had a 3D primary key that matched the foreign key on the child record and had a start date <= the query date and an end date >= query date. You could base the query on the current date, a date of interest, or a date on the child record. For example, if we were joining from a pay record to the pay parameters, then the query date would be the pay period date on the child record.

4.3.3.9   Reporting systems use temporal data extensively

A 3D ES is an online transaction processing (OLTP) database. How an OLTP database manages temporal data differs from an Online Analytical Processing (OLAP) database used for reporting and data warehouses. OLAP databases will take all data and time and slice it by period for ease of reporting. This allows reporting engines to see what all transactional and reporting data looked like at a given point in time. These databases will take non-temporal data and make it temporal for reporting. For example, you may see a contact record in the reporting database that identifies all the contacts' attributes at a given point of time (such as their age), so it can analyze this data against other temporal data and transactional data. Reporting databases should exist outside of an OLTP database.

4.3.3.10 Change history versus temporal
Temporal and change history data are not the same thing. Temporal data is time-sensitive data, whereas change history data is a log of what has changed about records, regardless of whether they are temporal.

For example, if a property tax system's assessment value is incorrect, we update the segment to reflect the correct assessment value. When the segment is updated, a change history record will be generated to identify who changed the record, using what means (menu option they used), other records affected in the same transaction, and a before and after image of what changed.

There is more about change history in the next section.

4.3.3.11 Functional components
The system provides data utilities that automatically maintain a temporal series. All the developer needs to do is provide parameters for the temporal update. Then, the utility will decide whether to create a new segment, update an existing one, merge two segments, insert a record series, or deactivate a segment. It will make these decisions based on the temporal resolution of the table. There are also utilities for setting up temporal data in the data conversion process.

4.3.3.12 Summary

It is critical for architects to understand the design of temporal data when systems are architected. There are many examples in the old paradigm where architects will make mistakes, such as making every table temporal or not and formally defining temporal methods, yet allowing developers to choose on a case-by-case basis how they want to manage temporal data.

The new paradigm system clearly distinguishes differences between temporal and change history data. Furthermore, it provides built-in utilities to manage data the same way in all 3D ESs. This will accelerate the development of systems that manage temporal data and make it possible for systems to exchange data, even if it is temporal.

4.3.4 Change history design

4.3.4.1 Overview

The change history module further supports the 3D ES time dimension. Change history represents an audit log of every change in the database. Change history needs to be transaction-based to track all changes that happen as a part of a transaction. Change history also needs to track changes for both temporal and non-temporal data.

4.3.4.2 Old paradigm methods of change history

In the old paradigm, we track change history via three main methods.

- **Case-by-case basis**. A developer will create history tables on a case-by-case basis. For example, you might see an Address History table or a Name History table. Each developer will do it their own way, and the change history will likely not be tied back to the user that caused the change.

- **Adding columns to every table**. It is common to see architects decide to add change history columns to every table in the system, such as UpdateDate, UpdatedBy, CreateDate, CreatedBy. This is certainly simple but also very limited. The main issues with this method are:
  - o When a user updates a record, you cannot see what changed.
  - o It is difficult to create a report that shows all additions and changes made by a given user.
  - o Even though records are updated many times, the UpdatedBy and UpdatedDate only provide information for the last user to make an update.

- **Shadow tables**. We store a snapshot of a record in a shadow table as soon as that record changes. Some database vendors provide this option, which is very resource intensive and difficult for reporting. Plus, it does not neatly tie back to the user that made the change.

How systems in the old paradigm choose to track change history go back to two main decisions. Are there composite primary keys? Did they create a data dictionary at the center of the architecture? If the answer is yes to either of these questions, creating a cost-effective and sophisticated change history system will not be possible. Even if the architects answer no to both questions, retrofitting an old paradigm system with a centralized change history system is not simple.

4.3.4.3   Features of change history in the new paradigm

Change history is one of the cornerstone features of 3D ESs. The features of the 3D ES change history system are:

- It is stored in a central location and manages change history data for all tables.

- It is as light as possible while updating master data. This is important because we do not want to slow down transactions or extend how long tables are locked.

- It links directly to the data dictionary.

- It is immutable (i.e., users cannot change it).

- We can use it to track changes caused by batch updates. For example, when multiple selected records have a common change applied simultaneously.

- It is parameterized so we can control:

o Which columns trigger change history records to get generated. For example, a table may have a 'current balance' column. If the 'current balance' on record changes, we generally do not want change history records to get generated because it creates extra overhead and does not provide useful information.

o Which tables are tracked, and for what database events (i.e., inserts, updates, and deletes).

o Which commands/menu options in the system get tracked.

- We can track commands/menu options even without data change. For example, we may need tracking every time we initiate a "View Pay Compensation" command.

- It tracks changes by transaction. For example, if a user edits a form, such as a member form containing a main record and many sub-records, the system will keep track of all updates that occur as a part of the update and group them in that transaction.

4.3.4.4 Viewing change history data

Authorized users can drill down and view change history data in four main ways:

- **View change history by record**. Users can drill down from any record in the system and see the complete history of changes (if we turn on change history). For example, you could drill down from a contact and view change history or drill down from a fixed asset and see change history. The user sees the following change history information:

- ○ Date and time the change history event occurred.
- ○ Which user caused the change history event.
- ○ Which command/menu option invoked the change.
- ○ A listing of all records in all tables impacted by the change. Included for each table is a before and after image of any changed columns. If the change is related to a foreign key, rather than showing that ID changing from one value to another, it will show the readable translation for the ID based on the data dictionary. For example, if a fixed asset was reclassified, rather than showing that the asset type changed from 123 to 321, it would show the asset type change from Truck to Gravel Truck.

- **View change history by command/menu option.** Users can drill down for a command/menu option and see all change history data generated from executing the command. The change history data includes before and after images of the record(s) impacted and the ID of the user who executed the command. For example, it is possible to drill down and view all instances where the "Change Password" command was executed.

- **View change history by column.** Users can drill down for a particular column and see all change history events, including a change to the column of interest. For example, it can show all change history events of employment status. We can then filter further to look at all change history events where employment status was changed by a specific user.

- **View change history by user.** Users can drill down and view all changes made by a particular user in the system. It can even track situations where they merely accessed a command and made no changes.

4.3.4.5   Undoing changes

Users can undo a change. This is particularly useful if it is a large, complex change that affects multiple tables or if it affects temporal data. For example, if a particular user was incorrectly making changes to the system, then the system can undo their changes. The undo process reverses all types of changes, including restoring deleted records or deleting added records. Before the system undoes a change, it verifies that there are no future changes to undo first. Also, the system generates a change history event when a change is undone. It is possible to view all situations where the undo feature was initiated. Of course, the ability to undo changes is for super users, those who understand the impact of undoing changes.

4.3.4.6   Not all data is tracked using change history

Change history mostly applies to master data and not to transactional data. A journal entry is an example of transactional data. When we create a journal entry, we are typically not tracking when it got created, updated, or deleted. This is because journal entries are like a log in themselves; once posting a journal entry, it cannot be updated.

There are also performance reasons for not tracking change history on transactional data. For example, it is not uncommon to generate hundreds of thousands of journal entries at a time for annual billing processes. You certainly do not want to bog the process down by creating a change history record for every record created.

If you need change history data for financial data, you can always limit when it gets generated. For example, you can limit change history events to only tracking changes when the journal entry is changed. You can further limit this to not generating a change history event if a particular column value changes, like the transaction status, so that batch approvals would not cause generating change history events for all transactions in the batch.

4.3.4.7   Change history is used for exporting updates to master data

When a change occurs to master data and the master data is subscribed to, a change history event will automatically be triggered. This change history event will be broadcast to all systems interested in the master data.

The users of subscriber systems can view a change history event before applying the update to their master data. If they choose to apply the update, the subscriber system records the original change history event.

The change history event is also used in subscriber systems to indicate an outstanding change that needs to be applied. For example, suppose a governor of a member record made an update that was broadcast to a subscriber system that had not yet applied the change. Then, when the user browses member data, the member record will highlight that a change history event can be applied.

4.3.4.8   Change history data for machine learning and AI

Change history data will be valuable input data for machine learning and AI routines. It can provide a record of what master data is changing, how frequently it changes, and who is making the change. The benefit of this data is that it is centralized for all types of data (mostly master data) and neatly classified by a data dictionary.

4.3.4.9   Benefits of a comprehensive change history

The benefits of an integrated change history mechanism that integrates with a master data exchange mechanism cannot be understated. Benefits include:

- **Ability to empower more users to update master data**. Without a sophisticated change history system, organizations will lock down updates to master data so master tables are updated correctly. A change history system tracks user updates to master data, so there is greater accountability for making the correct changes. As a result, users can update master data immediately rather than working around updating master data while waiting for a user with greater authority.

- **Users will quickly understand how a record goes to its current state**. Having a consistent change history mechanism that is readily available for all types of master data throughout a system allows users to quickly drill down and see the complete history that led to a record's current state. This is powerful information that helps a user to answer their own questions.

- **Assists support resources with debugging**. Change history data helps support resources in debugging issues that exist in the system. Support resources can retrace the steps of a user to reproduce errors.

- **Reduce development costs.** In the old paradigm, developers spend time designing and building change history systems into their applications. This represents a tremendous duplication of effort, which increases costs for development and maintenance. The new paradigm includes a powerful change history system augmented for specific business use cases.

4.3.4.10 Data model design

The data model below depicts the data entities and relationships in place to support change history.

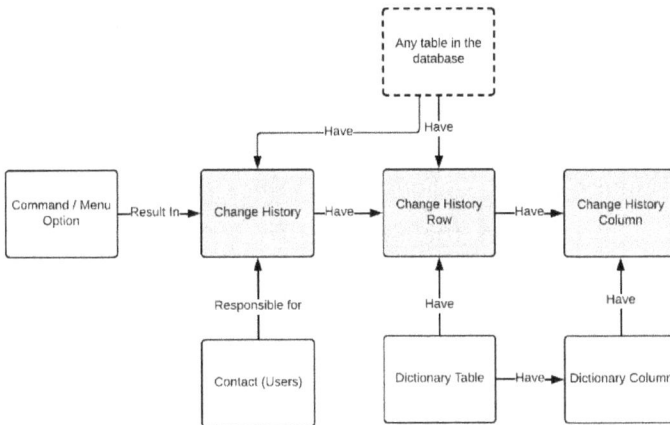

Menu/Command Option – The 3D ES framework has a table with all menu and command options a user can invoke. This table includes an indicator as to whether change history is tracked for a given menu/command option.

Change History – We create a change record anytime a change occurs. It identifies the command executed, the user that performed the change, and the date and time of the change.

Contact – Contacts represent any person or organization that an organization deals with in order to conduct business. Users are a type of contact.

Change History Row – A Change History Row record gets generated when a command/menu updates a table with change history turned on. This record connects to the original Change History record, the table impacted by the change, and the table/row id of the changed record. This record also includes a before and after image of the record, which is stored in a JSON format.

Dictionary Table – Dictionary Tables contain one record for each table in the system. This record contains an indicator for the change history system to tell whether logging should occur on inserts, updates, deletes, or not.

Dictionary Column – Dictionary Columns contain one record for each column in each table. It contains an indicator of whether a change to a column value will cause a change history event to occur.

Change History Column – This table contains a before and after image of any column whose value changed as a part of a table update. If the column is a foreign key column, then the translation for the foreign key is stored. For example, if a foreign key linked to the contact table changed from 123 to 321, it would look up the associated name for 123 and 321 and store that as well. This is to provide a user-friendly version of change history.

Any table in the database – Any table in the database can have change history turned on. This relationship is stored in a variable one-to-many and allows us to drill down from any record in the database to see the change history events.

4.3.4.11 Data dictionary
Below are the data dictionary elements for Change History.

Table Name	Column Name	DataType	Purpose
ChangeHistory	ID	BigInt	3D primary key
ChangeHistory	ContactIDUser	BigInt	Foreign key
ChangeHistory	CommandID	BigInt	Foreign key
ChangeHistory	DictionaryTableID-AppliesTo	BigInt	Multilink
ChangeHistory	RowIDAppliesTo	BigInt	Multilink
ChangeHistory	RowTemporalEndDate	Date	Data
ChangeHistory	ChangeDate	datetime	Data
ChangeHistory	IsExported	Boolean	Data
ChangeHistory	IsMaxRecordsIgnored	Boolean	Data
ChangeHistory	Comments	Varchar	Data
ChangeHistory	ChangeHistoryIdUndo	BigInt	Data
ChangeHistory	RowStatus	Char	System
ChangeHistoryRow	ID	BigInt	3D primary

Table Name	Column Name	DataType	Purpose
			key
ChangeHistoryRow	ChangeHistoryID	BigInt	Foreign key
ChangeHistoryRow	DictionaryTableID-AppliesTo	BigInt	Multilink
ChangeHistoryRow	RowIDAppliesTo	BigInt	Multilink
ChangeHistoryRow	RowTemporalEndDate	Date	Data
ChangeHistoryRow	ChangeDate	datetime	Data
ChangeHistoryRow	ActionType	Varchar	Data
ChangeHistoryRow	OperationType	Varchar	Data
ChangeHistoryRow	OldData	jsonb	Data
ChangeHistoryRow	NewData	jsonb	Data
ChangeHistoryRow	IsProcessed	Boolean	Data
ChangeHistory-Column	ID	BigInt	3D primary key
ChangeHistory-Column	ChangeHistoryRowID	BigInt	Foreign key
ChangeHistory-Column	DictionaryColumnID	BigInt	Foreign key
ChangeHistory-Column	DictionaryTableIDBefore	BigInt	Foreign key
ChangeHistory-Column	DictionaryTableIDAfter	BigInt	Foreign key
ChangeHistory-Column	RawDataBefore	Varchar	Data
ChangeHistory-Column	RawDataAfter	Varchar	Data
ChangeHistory-Column	TranslatedDataBefore	Varchar	Data
ChangeHistory-Column	TranslatedDataAfter	Varchar	Data

4.3.4.12 Functional components

Change History has the following functions.

- **Refresh triggers**. This function recreates the triggers for change history according to the data dictionary. Run this function anytime parameters are changed that affect change history. Examples of such changes are:
  o Turning change history on for a command.
  o Changing the scope of change history for a table (e.g., insert, update, delete).
  o Changing tracked columns.

- **Generate change history**. This function takes change history records created due to change history triggers and generates the Change History Column data. It provides a before and after image of any columns that changed. For foreign key references, the function will translate the foreign key based on the translation for the table specified in the data dictionary. For example, if the Contact ID changes from 123 to 321, the function would look up the name for 123 and 321 and capture the change. This information is helpful to users that need to see a user-friendly version of changes. This function also creates user-friendly versions of temporal changes. For example, if rate data was temporal and a rate changed from .05 to .06 effective Jan 1, 2020, its temporal records get inserted, updated, and deleted. To a user, seeing these temporal updates would not have much meaning. This function deciphers the data that changed and presents the user with a meaningful representation.

- **Change history undo**. This function undoes an existing change history record. That means all change history event updates will be reversed to their original state before the change occurs. In addition, the function will verify that there are no change history events that will need to be undone first. Change history undo events are tracked the same way as normal change history events.

4.3.4.13 User interface considerations

There are change history menu options in the utility menu. These menu options allow users to perform the following queries to view change history data:

- Show all change history events caused by a user.

- Show all change history events caused by a command/menu option.

- Show all change history events that affect a particular column.

Also, a change history browse can be connected to any browse list for records to see the associated change history for a given record. For example, view change history events for a contact.

4.3.4.14 Summary

Having a sophisticated change history module built into 3D ESs is mandatory. It provides users with critical information that allows them to be more efficient. It is one of the cornerstones that allow changes to master data to be broadcast to subscriber systems with an interest.

4.3.5 Master data exchange design

4.3.5.1 Overview

This section discusses the architecture for the master data exchange module. The key purpose of the master data exchange module is to securely exchange master data between 3D ESs. It is important to have master data consistent among systems so that transactional data is classified by the same master data. It allows rolling up data from systems for localities (e.g., regional systems, departmental systems, branch systems, and retail outlets) to the organization system. For example, there could be many healthcare entities (e.g., hospitals, labs, and clinics), each running a 3D ES in a healthcare environment. Data from each entity would roll up to the main healthcare entity for analysis.

Master data does not always have to be top-down, though. For example, in a government environment, the land registry will own land records and all departments interested in those records will be subscribers.

Master data governance is transferable. For example, in an association system with regional entities that provide services for members, a regional entity will govern the members they serve. Members can transfer from one regional entity to another. Master data exchange also allows suppliers to communicate with their customers. For example, in an oil and gas business, oil and gas service providers would subscribe to master data managed by the oil and gas company to allow the service provider to communicate service records and the related financial records to the oil and gas company.

4.3.5.2 Overview of the data exchange process

The data exchange process has three main components:

- **Export**. The export process reviews the subscriptions to master records and determines what to export. We export records because they are related to a new subscription or due to record updates.

- **Distribute**. The distribute process is responsible for getting master data updates to the right systems. It operates much like an email server.

- **Import**. The import process is responsible for receiving records from the distribute process and applying them to the database according to specified import rules.

4.3.5.3 Systems, subnet servers, and the master data server

There are three key terms related to exchanging master data between systems: systems, subnet servers, and the master data server.

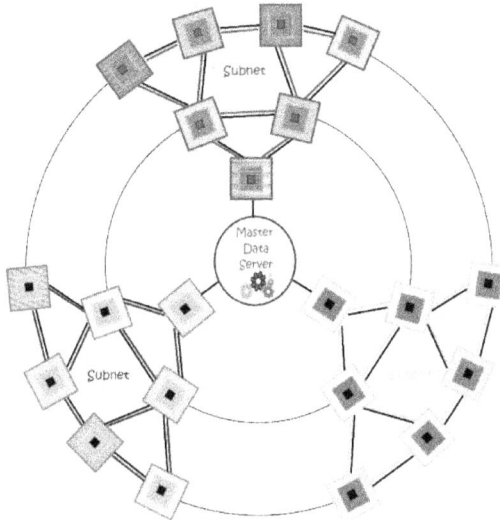

Systems are 3D ESs that meet the needs of a locality. Systems reside on a subnet server. There can be one or more systems on a subnet server. The following process occurs when a system publishes a master data update:

1. The system publishes the master data update to the subnet server, which instantaneously passes it to any systems that are subscribers and are operating on the same subnet server as the system publishing the data.

2. If the master data update is destined for a different subnet server(s), then the update is stored on the master data server.

3. Subnet servers will poll the master data server to see if there are any master data updates that they need to download. If there are, the subnet server will download the master update and pass it to systems that reside on that server.

4. The last step is for a system to process any master data updates passed to it for processing.

This works just like an email server. With an email server, a client can send an email to parties inside and outside of their organization. When they do so, an email is written to the local email server, which will instantaneously pass the message to any parties inside the organization. The email will be stored in the cloud if it is for a party outside the organization. Eventually, an email server will connect and download any email messages intended for parties on that server. Then it will pass the email message to the appropriate party.

4.3.5.4   Security

A primary concern is the communication of master data between subnet servers. There are five considerations for master data server security:

1. **Master data server contains limited data.** When a governor of master data broadcasts updates to subscriber systems, it creates a data package written to the master data server where subscriber systems pick it up. Once all subscribers have picked up their data packages, the server permanently removes the data package. This way only minimal master data packages will ever reside on the master data server at any given time.

2. **Master data generally is not that useful.** Even if a hacker gains access to an organization's master data updates on the master data server, it is generally uninteresting data. Mostly, it will be classification and lookup tables shared by all systems.

3. **Subnet design.** The subnet design allows a large organization to share all types of data on their subnet. That means this data never leaves their server. Data leaves their subnet server only when intended for a system that exists on a different subnet. There are controls to secure data shared through the master data server, but it is recommended not to share private data. For example, 3D ESs sharing contact information should do so on a local subnet, not on the master data server. It is perfectly acceptable if organizations wish to create their own custom code to share data.

4. **Applying updates from 3D ES data servers.** Users control how those updates get applied when an update to master data comes in from a 3D ES data server. For example, they can opt for automatic updates from trusted 3D ESs (e.g., if an update comes from the parent organization's 3D ES, then it is considered a trusted 3D ES), or they can opt to review every change before it is applied manually.

5. **Organizations will be responsible for transferring transactional data between systems.** There will be patterns and recommendations for moving transactional data between systems and rolling data up from regional 3D ESs to the central organization. Generally, these activities will be done on the subnet and will be the responsibility of the local organization to ensure that it is fully secure.

4.3.5.5 Scalability

The master data server sits at the center of all subnet servers and acts like an email server to exchange master data between governors and subscribers.

This has the potential to become a bottleneck, but there are two reasons why this should not be a concern:

- **Master data doesn't change very often.** Email servers exchange emails between servers without significant performance issues. Now consider how often master data changes, such as adding a GL account to a GL account structure or adding a new status to a transaction status table. It is generally infrequent. After broadcasting master data to subscriber systems, it will not change all that frequently. Certainly, far less volume than email servers manage.

- **Multiple master data servers can be created**. There is no reason we cannot have multiple data servers designed to exchange data between them. After all, this follows 3D ES principles.

4.3.5.6   Data model design

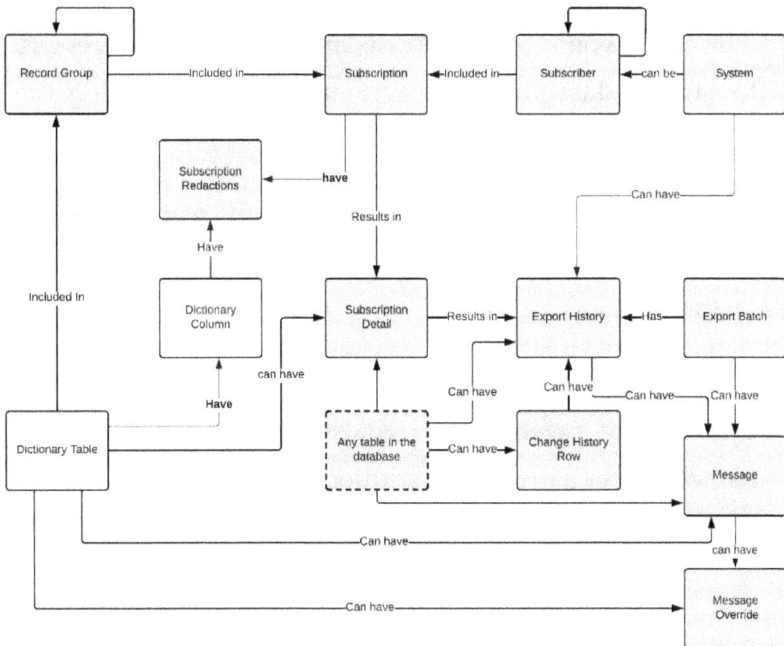

Record Group – hierarchical organization of tables involved in a group (e.g., contact -> address).

Subscription – defines subscriptions for master data. Specifies the subscriber and their subscription. Can be for all rows in a table or just one.

Subscriber – hierarchical grouping of systems that can subscribe to records (Retail Outlets -> Store A, Store B, Store C).

System – contains one record for every system encountered in a given systems database. For example, if a given system exchanges data with ten different systems, then there would be ten records in this table. It is necessary to capture data about the system so an organization can put a name to a system in which it interacts.

Subscription Detail – an expanded-out version of the subscriptions based on the record group and subscriber hierarchies.

Subscription Redaction – contains a record for each column that needs to be redacted. There can be many redactions for a given subscription.

Dictionary Table – contains one record for every table in a database.

Export History – organized into batches. Contains one record for every record included in a batch.

Change History Row – contains a before and after image of the record.

Message – identifies an error or warning message associated with an export history record. Messages are also linked to the export batch and their associated table.

Message override – identifies overrides to allow for ignoring warning messages.

4.3.5.7 Data dictionary

Below are the data dictionary elements for Data Exchange.

Table Name	Column Name	Data-Type	Purpose
Subscriber	ID	BigInt	3D primary key
Subscriber	SubscriberIDParent	BigInt	Foreign key
Subscriber	SystemID	BigInt	Foreign key
Subscriber	Name	Varchar	Data
Subscriber	DisplaySequence	Integer	System
Subscriber	TopDownLevel	Integer	System
Subscriber	RowStatus	Char	System
Subscriber	ChangeHistoryID	BigInt	Audit
RecordGroup	ID	BigInt	3D primary key
RecordGroup	RecordGroupIDParent	BigInt	Foreign key
RecordGroup	DictionaryTableID	BigInt	Foreign key
RecordGroup	DictionaryColumnID	BigInt	Foreign key
RecordGroup	Name	Varchar	Data
RecordGroup	WhereClause	Varchar	Data
RecordGroup	DisplaySequence	Integer	System
RecordGroup	TopDownLevel	Integer	System

Table Name	Column Name	Data-Type	Purpose
RecordGroup	RowStatus	Char	System
RecordGroup	ChangeHistoryID	BigInt	Audit
Subscription	ID	BigInt	3D primary key
Subscription	SubscriberID	BigInt	Foreign key
Subscription	RecordGroupID	BigInt	Foreign key
Subscription	RowIDSubscribedTo	BigInt	Data
Subscription	EffectiveDate	Date	Data
Subscription	ExpiryDate	Date	Data
Subscription	ChangeHistoryID	BigInt	Audit
Subscription-Detail	ID	BigInt	3D primary key
Subscription-Detail	SubscriptionID	BigInt	Foreign key
Subscription-Detail	SubscriberID	BigInt	Foreign key
Subscription-Detail	RecordGroupID	BigInt	Foreign key
Subscription-Detail	DictionaryTableID-SubscribedTo	BigInt	Multilink
Subscription-Detail	RowIDSubscribedTo	BigInt	Multilink
Subscription-Detail	RowStatus	Char	System
Subscription-Detail	ChangeHistoryID	BigInt	Audit
Subscription-Redaction	ID	BigInt	3D primary key
Subscription-Redaction	SubscriptionID	BigInt	Foreign key
Subscription-Redaction	DictionaryColumnID Redacted	BigInt	Foreign key

Table Name	Column Name	Data-Type	Purpose
Subscription-Redaction	RedactedSQL	Varchar	Data
Subscription-Redaction	RedactedValue	Varchar	Data
Subscription-Redaction	RedactedTranslation	Varchar	Data
Subscription-Redaction	RowStatus	Char	System
Subscription-Redaction	ChangeHistoryID	BigInt	Audit
History	SystemIDDestination	BigInt	Foreign key
History	Source	Char	Data
System	ID	BigInt	3D primary key
System	exDataServerID	BigInt	Foreign key
System	Name	Varchar	Data
System	SchemaName	Varchar	Data
System	ProductionVersion	Integer	Data
System	TestVersion	Integer	Data
System	SubscriptionKey	Varchar	Data
System	RowStatus	Char	System
System	ChangeHistoryID	BigInt	Audit
Message	ID	BigInt	3D primary key
Message	HistoryBatchID	BigInt	Foreign key
Message	HistoryID	BigInt	Foreign key
Message	DictionaryTableID	BigInt	Foreign key
Message	MessageID	BigInt	Foreign key
Message	MessageSeverity	Integer	Data
Message	IsOverridden	Boolean	Data
Message	Description	Varchar	Data
Message	ChangeHistoryID	BigInt	Audit

Table Name	Column Name	Data-Type	Purpose
Message-Override	ID	BigInt	3D primary key
Message-Override	DictionaryTableID	BigInt	Foreign key
Message-Override	MessageID	BigInt	Foreign key
Message-Override	Description	Varchar	Data
Message-Override	ChangeHistoryID	BigInt	Audit

4.3.5.8   Functional components

4.3.5.8.1   Managing record groups

This process allows a governor to create groupings of records that subscribers can access. A record group is hierarchical. An example of a one-level record group is a contact record. A two-level record group would be a contact and its address. The hierarchical design allows the record group to have as many levels as required. The record group includes a filtering capability. For example, you may wish only to share business addresses for a contact.

4.3.5.8.2   Defining subscriber groups

This process defines subscriber groups. Subscriber groups are in place to reduce the maintenance of subscriptions. For example, we can create a subscriber group for all hospitals. As soon as we add a new hospital to the group, it instantly inherits all the group's subscriptions. A subscriber group is hierarchical and can have as many levels as required.

4.3.5.8.3   Subscribing to records

This process allows a system to create a subscription to a master record. When we create a subscription, the following parameters exist:

Record Group – defines the record group that one subscribes.

Record – defines the record that one subscribes. If it is left null, all records in the table belong to the subscription.

Subscriber – defines the subscriber group for the subscription. There can be one or more systems in a subscriber group.

Effective date – defines the first date for the subscription.

Expiry date – defines the last active date for the subscription.

Subscriptions can be hierarchical. For example, the health care administrator could define a chart of accounts. This could be inherited by the region and then expanded. After that, a district within the region could inherit the chart of accounts from the region.

4.3.5.8.4   Redacting columns

When data is exported to another system, users require the ability to redact data. This can involve substituting the column with a new value, masking it, or setting it to a null value.

A simple example is redacting the salary column on a personnel record.

A more complex example is generalizing contact information. For example, instead of providing a foreign key reference to the actual staff member that performed an activity, it may be necessary to generalize it to the organization that the staff member works for.

4.3.5.8.5   Exporting records

The export process goes through the following steps to export data:

1. Generate subscription detail (SubscriptionDetail) based on the record group hierarchy, subscriber group hierarchy, and subscription. For example, if a record group was for a contact and address, and a subscriber group has two entities, we would create a subscription detail record for the contact and address record for both entities.

2. Next, the process identifies the records to be exported (History) based on the records involved in the subscription. For example, if a subscription was for an entire table, the process creates subscription detail records for each record. Another example would be if a contact had multiple address records, the process creates one subscription detail record for each address record. Note that when the process is evaluating records to include, it uses the filtering

clause to note if it exists. For example, we can limit address records to business address records.

3. One of the more complex situations this process handles is when a subscription is for a whole table and the record group includes child records from another table. The process will get all parent records and then the child records for that parent. The process can go down many levels because record groups are hierarchical.

4. The process checks if any change history records were generated since the last export. If a change is detected, it will be added to the export (History).

5. The process checks all foreign key references for any data being exported. The process will include that data for the records if there are foreign key references. The only columns included in the export are the header columns defined in the dictionary. The allowance for foreign keys is in place, so bad foreign key references are not created in the subscriber systems.

6. The data is all packaged up and sent to the distribution process.

4.3.5.8.6   Distributing records

Each subnet server has a distribution process responsible for distributing records to the subscriber systems. It does this in three phases:

1. Retrieve from the master data server any data packages that are for the subnet server that it is running on.

2. Distribute data to the local systems (i.e., the systems that reside on the same subnet that the distribution process runs on).

3. Create data packages and place them on the master data server for any external subnets.

We illustrate this process through the following example:

- System 1000 on subnet 1 is a governor system. The users on that system make some updates to subscription data that cause the export of master data. Some of the exported master data is going to systems on subnet 1, and the remaining data is going to other subnets.

- The distribution process starts by going to the master data server to check and see if there are any master data packages for subnet 1. It finds some and then combines it with the master data updates that System 1000 created.

- Then it sends the updates to local systems on Subnet 1.

- Next, it creates packages for each subnet receiving data and places these updates on the master data server.

- The distribution process for those subnet servers will pick up the packages and distribute them to their local systems.

The distribution process is the only process with permission to read and place packages on the master data server.

4.3.5.8.7 Importing records

This process runs on a system responsible for accepting updates from the distribution process and then applying them to its database. It has two levels of error checking. The first phase checks for structural differences in tables updated between the subscriber and governor systems, and the second stage of error checking occurs when processing the records.

The process can have error messages or warning messages. Users can override warning messages on a one-time basis or set up permanent overrides. For example, if the import process detects a new column in a table, the user can opt to set up a default for that column and then permanently ignore that message in the future. Once no error conditions exist, the import batch can be applied to the database.

The types of error conditions that are checked for are as follows:

Error conditions:

- The process uses the built-in capabilities of the database to catch integrity errors. The errors are caught, stored in the database with the batch, and reported to the user. Examples of error conditions are as follows:

  o Violated foreign key constraint.
  o Violated null constraint.
  o Violated unique constraint.

Warning conditions:

- Source data from the governor has a column that does not exist on the subscriber database. This situation is a warning condition the user must acknowledge before the update can proceed.

- Destination table in the subscriber database has a column that exists but does not exist in the governor database. In this situation, as long as the column does not have a null constraint or there is a default value for the column, the error is just a warning message.

- Subscriber has updated the record since the last update from the governor. For example, if a record was received from a governor and then updated locally, the user receives a notification of the next update to the record. Subscribers need the ability to update locally when they need to proceed with internal processes and cannot wait for the governor to make the update and circulate.

We can customize the system with special rules for importing data. Some examples of rules are:

- If a specific system sends a master data update, then automatically apply it.

- If a column value changes on a table, then cause other actions to occur. For example, if the status of a person changes to deceased, then add an action item to a table to send a letter.

The import process can handle all types of updates from a governor. It can handle updates to temporal record series and insert, delete, and update records.

4.3.5.9 User interface considerations

The user can browse batches of master data updates to import. The user will have the following options:

- **Process an import batch.** When they process the batch, they can process records if there are only warning conditions. If there are error messages, the user can change the database (such as setting up a default value for a not null column) and then re-process the batch.

- **View errors associated with the batch.** For a given warning message, the user can do a one-time override or a permanent override.

- **View import records in the batch before and after images of changed columns.** The user can flag an update as "ignore" to process the rest of the batch.

When the user is browsing data in the system, highlight the record if applying an outstanding update. For example, a user could be viewing data for oil and gas wells and see a highlighted oil and gas well row because the governor had made an update that the user had not yet applied.

4.3.5.10 Summary

The Master Data Module allows data to be easily exchanged securely between systems with no programming. Users can define what master data needs to be shared and which systems require this master data. The Master Data Module takes care of distributing this data when it is first subscribed to and then sending updates when things change.

The Master Data Module is robust and eliminates almost all programming associated with exchanging master data between systems. Having said that, if a particular system has specialized needs for master data exchange that go beyond the capabilities of the Master Data Module, the team can recreate these functions in custom code.

4.3.6 Record governance design

4.3.6.1 Overview

Governance exists so that users always know which system holds the gold standard version of a given master record. By default, when a system creates a record, it will automatically govern that record. Likewise, when a system imports a record from another system, it will, by default, not govern that record. So explicitly tracking which system has governance over which records is not necessary for a system's vast majority of records. Governance is implicitly based on the System ID portion of the 3D primary key.

What we do track with the record governance module are the exceptions. Governance records get generated that override the default rules. For example, if a system created a master record but then transferred the record governance to another system, governance override records would exist in the old governor and new governor systems and on the master data server.

Record governance can apply to a single record or a group of records. For example, if a system governs a contact, it will likely also govern the address associated with the contact.

4.3.6.2 Data model design

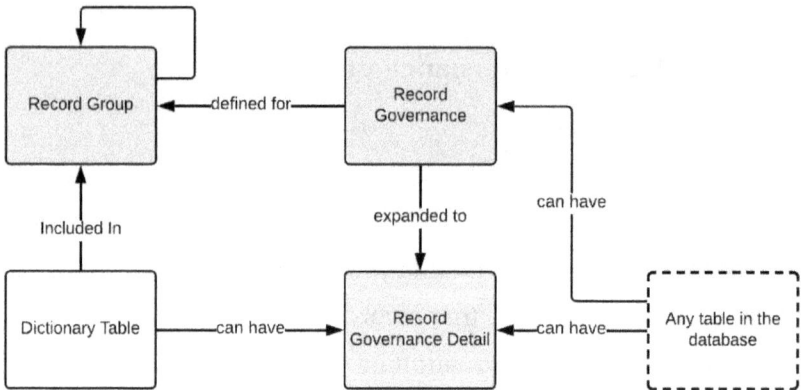

Record Group – Defines hierarchical groups of records.

Dictionary Table – Have one row for each table in the system.

Record Governance – Defines record governance for a record group.

Record Governance Detail – Expanded detail of the record governance record.

4.3.6.3 Data dictionary

Below are the data dictionary elements for Record Governance.

Table Name	Column Name	Data-Type	Purpose
Governance	ID	BigInt	3D primary key
Governance	SystemID	BigInt	Foreign key
Governance	RecordGroupID	BigInt	Foreign key
Governance	RowIDSubscribedTo	BigInt	Data
Governance	IsTransferred	Boolean	Data
Governance	TransferDate	Date	Data
Governance	ChangeHistoryID	BigInt	Audit
Governance-Detail	ID	BigInt	3D primary key
Governance-Detail	GovernanceID	BigInt	Foreign key
Governance-Detail	SystemID	BigInt	Foreign key
Governance-Detail	RecordGroupID	BigInt	Foreign key
Governance-Detail	DictionaryTableID-SubscribedTo	BigInt	Multilink
Governance-Detail	RowIDSubscribedTo	BigInt	Multilink
Governance-Detail	ChangeHistoryID	BigInt	Audit

4.3.6.4   Functional components

4.3.6.4.1   Record governance transfer

This function causes record governance for a given record to get transferred from one system to another. Invoking this function will:

- Create a record governance override on the originating system in a pending state.

- Create an update on the master data server to indicate a pending transfer.

- Create a governance transfer record to export to the system receiving governance.

When the receiving system accepts the transfer, the status will be flagged as completed on the master data server and the originating system.

4.3.6.4.2   Record governance revoke

The originating system can use this function to revoke a transfer if the recipient system has not accepted the transfer. This will cause a governance revoke transaction to be logged on the master data server and an update to the recipient system governance override record.

4.3.6.5   User interface considerations

Users can inquire about any record in the system to see which system holds governance for a record. Users can also view the governance transfer history for any record. This will show them any governance transfers initiated, revoked, or approved.

4.3.6.6   Summary

The Record Governance Module manages the transfer of record governance between systems. It ensures that no two systems have record governance at one time. It also helps users to recognize which system has governance so that it can be requested if it is needed.

4.3.7 Financial system design

4.3.7.1 Overview

The design of the financial system is paramount to how effective it will be for organizations to track their finances. In this section, we cover the high-level design of the financial system. We look at the design of most old paradigm financial systems and how it affects their flexibility. Then we look at the core financial system's design for 3D ESs and the anticipated benefits.

4.3.7.2 Old paradigm financial systems

Of course, we have had great success with financial systems because almost every business has a financial system implemented at an affordable price. Having said that, this section evaluates the three architectural issues that exist within the core design of most old paradigm financial systems.

4.3.7.2.1 Architecture of general ledger and sub-ledgers

The first architectural issue with many old paradigm financial systems is the concept of generating journal entries in a sub-ledger and then copying them to the general ledger.

In many cases with old paradigm financial systems, the general ledger and sub-ledgers are separate modules, even possibly separate systems. The sub-ledgers will evaluate operational data, formulate journal entries, and export them to the general ledger.

Three key issues that result from the general ledger/sub-ledger architectural design are:

- **Unable to link operational data with the related financial journal entries.** It is not possible to drill down from operational data and view the related journal entries. For example, it is not possible to drill down from a data entity like an oil well, and view all asset, expense and revenue journal entries. If the requirement exists, a separate account for each oil well is created, proliferating GL accounts and representing data duplication that must be continually maintained. Furthermore, it means that users cannot easily produce financial statements based on attributes of a data entity, such as producing a financial statement in an oil system based on the type of the well.

- **Timeliness of data.** When a sub-ledger creates journal entries for a general ledger, it evaluates the operational data and generates journal entries for the general ledger. The challenge begins when the operational data changes after generating journal entries. Some sub-ledgers cannot create adjusting entries, so they create manual journal entries. The second challenge comes when many sub-ledgers copy data into the general ledger. These two challenges cause accountants to delay applying sub-ledgers until the very last moment.

Accountants do this to minimize adjustments and ensure that conflicting inputs do not throw off the books. The delays with applying updates from sub-ledgers to general ledgers mean that the general ledgers are not up to date until applying all sub-ledgers, which, in some cases, is once per month.

*   **Issues with discrepancies between the general ledger and subledger systems**. As soon as you take data from one system and duplicate it in another you create an issue with keeping the two synchronized. As a result, getting one number from the general ledger and a different one from a sub-ledger is not uncommon. The challenge is to know which one you can trust. Staff may spend many hours trying to understand why there are differences in the numbers. This issue results from having two copies of the same data and being able to change one copy without replicating the change in the other. For example, an adjusting entry inserted in the general ledger without reflecting the same change in the sub-ledger, or operational data can change without reflecting the adjustment in the general ledger.

4.3.7.2.2   One-dimension GL account codes

The second architectural issue with many old paradigm systems is the design of GL account codes. GL account codes will often include components that hierarchically break down an account from a high-level classification (such as asset, liability, expense, or revenue), right down to a unique identifier for the account. Sometimes, GL Account codes will include components for data entities such as projects, assets, or oil and gas wells. In addition, GL account codes can include components to identify the business entity (i.e., cost center) related to the GL account.

Having all these components in a GL account code can result in a significant proliferation of GL accounts. This makes it difficult to restructure the GL account hierarchy, particularly if the GL account code has been used as a foreign key link to the GL account throughout the system.

4.3.7.2.3 Year-end closing process

The third architectural issue is related to how many old paradigm financial systems close out year-end. The goal of the year-end process is to zero out all revenue and expense accounts and create an entry to "Retained Earnings – Prior Period," which represents the net income for the year.

Old paradigm financial systems accomplish this by creating a closing journal entry for every revenue and expense account, that causes the balance of the account to be zero. Next, a journal entry is created that represents the total of all closing entries created in the previous step. This journal entry is changed to 'retained earning prior period', representing the year's net income. While this may seem simple enough, it creates superfluous entries that we must ignore during reporting. This can become an issue if the system has thousands of GL accounts due to a one-dimensional GL account number.

4.3.7.3   New paradigm financial system

The financial model within 3D ESs is designed to deal with the issues with old paradigm financial systems. It will track finances for large organizations and small organizations alike. The greatest power of this financial model is its ability to connect financial and operational data. With the 3D ES, architects can work with business users to decide how to connect journal entries to operational data.

For example, a project-based organization may link journal entries to projects for specific GL accounts. This would allow them to view all revenues and direct expenses related to a project. Other examples of linking journal entries to operational data are:

- Oil and gas company linking the asset, revenue, and expense transactions to oil and gas wells.

- Linking asset journal entries for capital expenditure, revenue, and expenses (including depreciation) to the related asset.

- Municipality relating revenues and expenses to parcels of land.

- Linking payroll journal entries to the staff member.

This capability does not just apply to master records but also to transactional records. For example, an organization that provides educational services could choose to have educational revenues sub-classified by course registration. This allows the organization to view all journal entries related to course registration, including invoice charges, adjustments, and reversals. It also allows the organization to analyze course profitability by the person taking the course, characteristic of the person (gender), course profitability, or characteristic of the course (full-time, part-time).

4.3.7.3.1   Normalized GL account and GL cost center data

Rather than using a one-dimensional GL account code, the new paradigm system breaks this data into the following normalized components:

- **GL account**. An old paradigm GL account contains data that expresses how a GL account fits into a hierarchy. The new paradigm system normalizes this data and sets up an actual GL account hierarchy with inherent capabilities for rolling data from the lowest to the highest levels. Users can reorganize the hierarchy and add new levels without affecting the underlying journal entries.

- **GL cost center**. The GL cost center structure is also hierarchical. In small organizations, only one cost center will represent the main organization. In large organizations, we can organize thousands of cost centers into a hierarchy with many levels.

- **Sub-classification by database entity**. As previously mentioned, any database entity can sub-classify journal entries. This is driven based on the GL account. For example, receivable and payable accounts are sub-classified by billing accounts connected to a contact record. Other examples include sub-classifying journal entries by assets, land parcels, or projects.

The features that are possible as a result of normalizing this data are:

- **Being able to drill down and analyze data at any level of the GL account or cost center hierarchies**. For example, a user could see a hierarchical view of the income statement with numbers presented at every level, then select a GL account such as salaries and see a hierarchical breakdown by cost center that shows salaries for the organization and each level in the hierarchy below.

- **Being able to produce financial statements for database entities or attributes of database entities**. For example, it will be possible to produce a financial statement for an oil and gas well or some combination of attributes for oil and gas wells, such as location and well status.

4.3.7.3.2 Communicating journal entries between organizations

One of the key goals of new paradigm systems is to enter data once and use it many times. The new paradigm financial system supports this goal on a macro basis by allowing one organization to create journal entries for another. This could be suppliers creating journal entries for their customers or organizations creating journal entries for their partners. The four features that support this goal are:

- **GL account inheritance.** The new paradigm principles allow us to define a GL account structure that is common to all organizations, then inherit and expand on that GL account structure for an industry, then inherit and expand on that structure for an organization, and finally inherit and expand on that for a regional entity of the organization. This will result in common 3D primary keys used for the same accounts in different systems. This will help organizations generate expense journal entries for their customers while simultaneously generating revenue journal entries for themselves.

- **Automated master data management.** Automated master data management allows us to share master data between organizations. For example, this will help an organization create a transaction for their partner or customer and connect the journal entry to the appropriate master record.

- **QR codes.** Not all master data will be shared via automated master data management. Sometimes we use QR codes (or something similar). For example, an oil and gas well service provider could wand in a QR code for a well they are servicing, and then create journal entries for their customer that are connected to the correct oil and gas well.

- **General ledger/sub-ledger.** An organization with the new paradigm can still use sub-ledgers and general ledgers. In fact, the new paradigm system includes built-in features for exporting data to an old paradigm general ledger.

It also allows creating separate new paradigm systems for general and sub-ledgers that share financial and operational data. The key difference between the new and old paradigm general ledger is that the new paradigm general ledger is capable of hosting all the master and transactional data that journal entries can be subclassified to. It can even be organized more like a reporting database containing denormalized views created strictly to analyze financial data. For example, suppose journal entries for an education business were linked to course registrations which were denormalized to contain attributes of the registrant, instructor, and course. In this case, financial statements could be produced by any of the attributes from the denormalized view, such as profitability by gender of the registrant.

4.3.7.3.3   Time-sensitive analysis of financial data

New paradigm financial systems offer a time dimension for analyzing finances by operational data. As a result of the operational system managing data using standardized temporal methods, it becomes possible to analyze finances by the version of the temporal data that was applicable when the journal entry took place. For example, if we were analyzing taxation revenues by the attributes of the land parcel, then the attributes would appear based on what was applicable at the time of the journal entry.

4.3.7.3.4   Aggregation of regional data

Detailed data from regional systems can be rolled up to the organizational level and used for analyzing finances. For example, in a membership system, detailed membership data could be rolled up from all regions and then used to analyze membership revenues.

4.3.7.3.5   Improved timeliness of data

We design the general ledger in the new paradigm to accommodate any data a sub-ledger can manage. As a result, there will no longer be a need to host data in a separate sub-ledger and then export it to the general ledger from time to time. The new paradigm general ledger will access posted and pending transactions typically held in the sub-ledgers until posted. For example, we can extend the financial system to allow creating purchase orders as temporary invoices, which can then be adjusted when the invoice is received. These two features combined will help users get an accurate prediction of the future finances.

4.3.7.3.6   Open-source model

The new paradigm is an open-source model that provides a core financial system that we can build upon. This will allow building new functionality only once and sharing with any organization that has adopted the new paradigm. As a result, it will reduce costs for the financial system while increasing the number of features available for adoption.

4.3.7.3.7   Budgeting

From a data perspective, budget records are very similar to journal entries. A budget entry is charged to an account and cost center for a given period. Budget entries can also be charged to entities within the enterprise model. A budget entry can relate to an asset, a project, or an oil and gas well.

Revisions to the budget lead to new budget entries that may add to budget entries, reverse existing ones, or make positive or negative adjustments to existing budget entries. The core new paradigm system includes features for budgeting.

4.3.7.3.8   Reporting period

Although we analyze finances by transaction date, sometimes finances need to be analyzed by reporting period. For example, an organization may receive an annual charge that applies to all reporting periods for the year. In this case, there is a transaction date based on the invoice date plus twelve journal entries, each with a different reporting period date.

4.3.7.3.9   Support multi-currency including bitcoin

One of the features to add to the core model is the ability to support multi-currency, including bitcoin. Bitcoin will require additional business rules as it is expressed in an 8-decimal number. For transactions and balance sheets to properly balance to zero, special rounding rules will be included in the core financial system. In the old paradigm, architects would have to figure out these rules on a system-by-system basis. In the new paradigm, it will be done once at a core level.

4.3.7.3.10   Exception reporting

A big part of analyzing finances is understanding the exceptions. Examples of such exceptions are:

- Getting charged twice for something.

- Missing a charge or revenue.

- Seeing an account balance go up or down significantly.

The financial system will identify these exceptions and allows users to drill down and quickly find out the cause.

4.3.7.4   Anticipated benefits

- **Improve timeliness of data**. The new paradigm will improve the timeliness of financial data by eliminating timing issues associated with sub-ledgers. Also, the new paradigm will generate journal entries as soon as purchase orders are approved, thereby increasing timeliness due to not having to wait for invoices to be received before updating the financial records.

- **Improve ability to analyze financial data**. In most old paradigm general ledger financial systems, we analyze financial data by GL account and cost center. The new paradigm is designed from the ground up to include two new dimensions: table object and time. Table object is multi-dimensional in that financial statements can be produced based on any row in any table in the system (e.g., project, oil well, fixed asset, etc.). Financial statements can also be produced based on the attributes of those entities (e.g., gas wells versus oil wells). The time dimension is possible because the new paradigm fully supports temporal data. So, if journal entries connect to temporal objects, then analysis of financial data can be time-sliced based on temporal versions of the records.

- **Improve efficiency for financial accounting.** The administration of the financial system will be simplified and made more efficient due to the following improvements:

  o   Eliminating sub-ledgers and the associated challenges with balancing.

  o   More automation will be available for generating transactions due to sharing source code from a common data structure.

  o   Fewer accounts will be needed to connect journal entries to entities in the enterprise database. This change effectively eliminates the need for object qualifiers in accounts.

  o   The new paradigm is designed to exchange data between systems, including financial transactions. It will eliminate the need for recreating these entries manually.

- **Simplify the process of identifying exceptions.** Finances have many recurring patterns that exist, which are similar to your personal finances. In your personal finances, you will see recurring expenses and income entries. The 3D ES includes features to search for broken patterns in the finances. An example of a broken pattern is an expense that occurs at roughly a consistent amount but is double one month implying the organization has been charged twice. Another example is a revenue amount that occurs consistently but is zero for one month. The 3D ES can identify many different types of anomalies in the finances as a built-in feature

- **Reduce costs with more features**. The new paradigm is an open-source model that provides a core financial system for us to build upon. We build new functionality once and share it with any organization adopting the new paradigm. In addition, it will reduce costs for the financial system while increasing the number of features available to be adopted. It will also allow organizations to rapidly change the financial system to meet its specific needs.

- **Improve audit trails**. The new paradigm includes a central audit trail that tracks all changes to all data. The neatly organized audit trail allows auditors to view change history from various perspectives. This feature is particularly valuable for changes to enterprise data that cause adjustments to financial entries.

4.3.7.5   Summary

All of the principles and architectural design for the new paradigm have led me to create a new 3D ES that will dramatically improve the efficiency of managing finances and its reporting capabilities.

The new paradigm will empower teams to extend financial systems using custom and open-source improvements. As a result, it will significantly benefit organizations that must respond quickly to new competitive advantages.

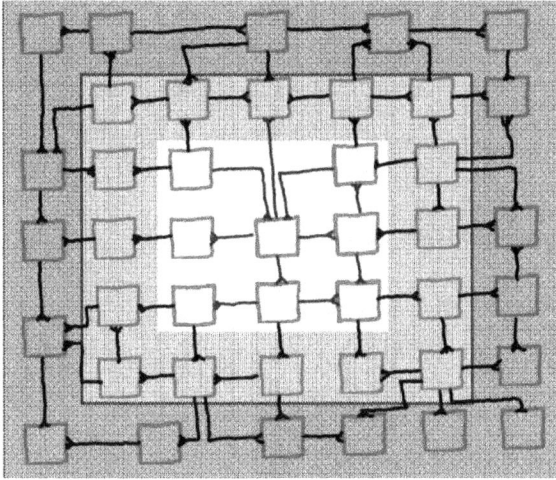

5 Core Data Models

5.1 Introduction

This section describes the first five core data models: Contact, Finance, Fixed Asset, Human Resources, and Activities. It is the first five illustrated in this book, however, we continue to develop additional core models in subject areas such as contract management and purchasing. All of these would be published to the centrally accessible and approved core models area shared as an open-source resource.

We design the core models to be expandable to meet specific business needs. We accomplish this primarily through creating subtypes for existing entities. However, it also works to add attributes to the existing core models.

New subtypes automatically inherit all the framework features, such as change history and master data management. This design approach allows for contextually malleable core models, that companies can extend to meet their specific needs.

The core models allow organizations to communicate based on their data. As a result, organizations can efficiently exchange data based on contacts, fixed assets, finances, personnel, and activities.

5.2 Contact registry

5.2.1 Overview

A contact registry is at the center of the enterprise database for the new paradigm. The contact registry is a central registry for all contacts for the organization and integrates with every other 3D ES module.

The contact module captures basic contact information for organizations, people, and groups such as committees. It can manage postal addresses, email addresses, phone numbers, relationships between contacts, alternate names, and alternate contact keys.

We can add subtypes to any contact type, adding additional details specific to that subtype. For example, if a contact is a member of an association, then additional details would be captured that are specific to a member.

Contact subtypes can be set up as temporal (time-sensitive) records showing how the contact data changes over time. We track any changes to contact data (temporal or non-temporal) in change history. Users can drill down for a given contact and see its complete change history.

One of the key benefits of the contact model design is that new contact types automatically inherit all the features connected to a contact. For example, a billing account (receivable/payable) connects to a contact. As a result, any new contact subtype can have a billing account.

5.2.2 Data model design

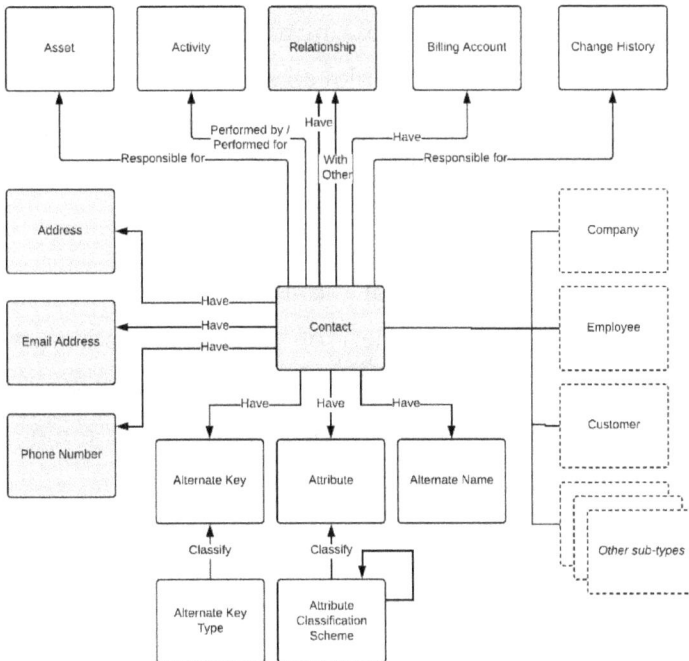

5.2.2.1   Contact

At the core of the contact model is an entity to capture information about contacts. A contact can be a person or an organization. A contact will always have a name and, if it is a person, will have other attributes such as first name, middle name, last name, birthdate, gender, salutation, etc.

Contacts have subtypes. Examples of subtypes for contacts are employee, customer, vendor, student, member, institution, etc. During 3D ESs design, we add subtypes to meet the organization's needs. A contact can be of more than one subtype. For example, a contact could be an employee and a member.

Subtypes share the same 3D primary key as the contact record. For example, an employee will have a record in the contacts table with a particular ID. This same ID will identify their record in the employee table.

5.2.2.2   Address

Postal addresses are one of the more complex entities to standardize because a variety of address formats exist in different parts of the world. There are even addresses that are textual descriptions of a property. To accommodate this requirement, a text blob is used to describe the address (AddressText).

An address service will be called to validate the address and return the address components in a standardized manner. Furthermore, the address service will correct the address if it is wrong and provide alternatives if unsure. Centralizing all addresses for all contacts in this manner also allows scanning the addresses from time to time to update postal code and city name changes.

Postal addresses include the ability for one contact to inherit the address from another and override components (e.g., employees inherit the address of their employer). We classify postal addresses by type (e.g., home, business).

5.2.2.3   Email address
This entity is for managing information about a contact's email addresses. It has basic information, including the email address and type (e.g., home or business).

5.2.2.4   Phone number
A contact can have many phone numbers. An address type classifies them (e.g., home or business).

5.2.2.5   Relationship
The relationship entity tracks relationships between two entities in the contact registry. This entity is temporal as it is in place for a specific period of time. The relationship entity is a registry for all types of relationships in which an entity may be involved. Employee/employer, president, board member, and educational institute/student are examples of relationships.

The subtyping of relationships allows for capturing more significant details about a particular type of relationship that do not apply to all other relationship types. An example of a situation for subtyping would be extending the attributes for employment to include other attributes.

The relationship entity is used instead of a contact type. This is because when data gets aggregated in a central location, you will see that a contact type becomes relative to the entity that provided the contact. For example, a person may be a staff member of a hospital, but when you aggregate the data in one place, it is not meaningful to know they have a contact type of staff member. Instead, you need to know a staff member of a particular hospital.

5.2.2.6   Alternate key

It is not uncommon to have multiple alternate keys to identify a contact. The alternate key provides a mechanism for users to dynamically define new keys to access data without making any system changes. For example, the users of a system may create an alternate key which is a customer key from another system. As a result, users can record the key for the customer and then access it using a built-in search mechanism.

5.2.2.7   Attribute

The attribute entity can be set up for an entity in the database. It allows attributes to be dynamically created by users and applied to any contact type. The attribute classification scheme defines the attributes that can be applied to a contact. It is a hierarchical scheme that breaks down attributes into categories. Examples using contact attributes include:

- Recording a skill inventory and then checking off all contacts that possess that skill.

- Creating mailing lists and then checking off all contacts that participate in that mailing list.

5.2.2.8   Alternate name
This entity manages alternate names for a contact. A contact can have zero or more alternate names.

5.2.2.9   Activity
Activities can be performed for a contact and/or performed by a contact.

5.2.2.10   Billing account
A contact can have zero or more billing accounts (e.g., receivable/payable).

5.2.2.11   Change history
A contact is responsible for initiating events that cause change history to be produced. Change history represents an audit log of changes to records in the system.

A contact also has change history related to it that represents all the changes to a contact's data since it was first created.

5.2.2.12   Fixed asset
A contact can be assigned responsibility for an asset.

5.2.3 Data dictionary

Below are the data dictionary elements for the Contact Registry. Only the core tables appear.

Table Name	Column Name	Data-Type	Purpose
Contact	ID	BigInt	3D primary key
Contact	ContactID	BigInt	Foreign key
Contact	LanguageID	BigInt	Foreign key
Contact	SalutationID	BigInt	Foreign key
Contact	BirthDate	Date	Data
Contact	Comments	Varchar	Data
Contact	ContactNumber	Varchar	Data
Contact	ContactPerson	Varchar	Data
Contact	FirstName	Varchar	Data
Contact	LastName	Varchar	Data
Contact	MiddleName	Varchar	Data
Contact	Name	Varchar	Data
Contact	PreferredFirstName	Varchar	Data
Contact	PreviousLastName	Varchar	Data
Contact	Website	Varchar	Data
Contact	RowStatus	Char	System
Contact	ChangeHistoryID	BigInt	Audit
ContactSubType-Employee	ID	BigInt	3D primary key
ContactSubType-Employee	Employment-StatusID	BigInt	Foreign key
ContactSubType-Employee	Employment-StartDate	Date	Data
ContactSubType-Employee	Comments	Varchar	Data
ContactSubType-	Employment-	Date	Data

Table Name	Column Name	Data-Type	Purpose
Employee	EndDate		
ContactSubType-Employee	TemporalStartDate	Date	Temporal
ContactSubType-Employee	TemporalEndDate	Date	Temporal
ContactSubType-Employee	RowStatus	Char	System
ContactSubType-Employee	ChangeHistoryID	BigInt	Audit
ContactSubType-User	ID	BigInt	3D primary key
ContactSubType-User	Login	Varchar	Data
ContactSubType-User	Password	Varchar	Data
ContactSubType-User	RowStatus	Char	System
ContactSubType-User	ChangeHistoryID	BigInt	Audit
Address	ID	BigInt	3D primary key
Address	comCityID	BigInt	Foreign key
Address	AddressID-InheritedFrom	BigInt	Foreign key
Address	AddressTypeID	BigInt	Foreign key
Address	ContactID	BigInt	Foreign key
Address	AddressText	Varchar	Data
Address	Additional-Information	Varchar	Data
Address	Address1	Varchar	Data
Address	Address2	Varchar	Data
Address	Address3	Varchar	Data
Address	Address4	varchar	Data
Address	City	Varchar	Data
Address	ProvinceState	Varchar	Data
Address	Country	Varchar	Data

Table Name	Column Name	Data-Type	Purpose
Address	EffectiveDate	Date	Data
Address	IsPrimaryAddress	Boolean	Data
Address	PostalZip	Varchar	Data
Address	LatLong	Float	Data
Address	RowStatus	Char	System
Address	ChangeHistoryID	BigInt	Audit
Email Address	ID	BigInt	3D primary key
Email Address	AddressTypeID	BigInt	Foreign key
Email Address	ContactID	BigInt	Foreign key
Email Address	Email	Varchar	Data
Email Address	IsPrimary	Boolean	Data
Email Address	RowStatus	Char	System
Email Address	ChangeHistoryID	BigInt	Audit
Phone Number	ID	BigInt	3D primary key
Phone Number	AddressPhone-TypeID	BigInt	Foreign key
Phone Number	AddressTypeID	BigInt	Foreign key
Phone Number	ContactID	BigInt	Foreign key
Phone Number	IsPrimary	Boolean	Data
Phone Number	Phone	Varchar	Data
Phone Number	RowStatus	Char	System
Phone Number	ChangeHistoryID	BigInt	Audit
Relationship	ID	BigInt	3D primary key
Relationship	ContactID1	BigInt	Foreign key
Relationship	ContactID2	BigInt	Foreign key
Relationship	RelationshipTypeID	BigInt	Foreign key
Relationship	Description	Varchar	Data
Relationship	Comments	Varchar	Data

Table Name	Column Name	Data-Type	Purpose
Relationship	TemporalStartDate	Date	Temporal
Relationship	TemporalEndDate	Date	Temporal
Relationship	RowStatus	Char	System
Relationship	ChangeHistoryID	BigInt	Audit

5.2.4 User interface considerations

- **Find duplicate.** There is a focus on keeping the contact registry free of duplicates. When a user adds a new contact, search functions will be available to help the user assess whether the contact already exists. It will list possible duplicate contacts by checking a combination of first name, last name, birthdate, email address, and phone number.

- **Merge duplicate.** If a duplicate contact does get in the registry, a merge function will be available to merge a contact record into an existing contact record.

5.3 Fixed asset registry

5.3.1 Overview

Another commonly encountered type of data for all types of organizations is fixed assets. Fixed assets such as land, buildings, and equipment (assets) are purchased for long-term use and are not likely to be converted quickly into cash. One of the key benefits of having the fixed asset registry as one of the core models is that it sets up the ability to move assets and related data between 3D ESs. For example, in a health care environment, assets could be rolled up to the highest level and be visible to all entities. Suppose a healthcare entity required an asset that another healthcare provider wasn't using. In that case, the asset transfers to the new entity along with the detailed data (such as maintenance records) and governance for maintaining the asset data.

5.3.2 Data model design

Below is the structure for the fixed asset module and a description for each of the entities.

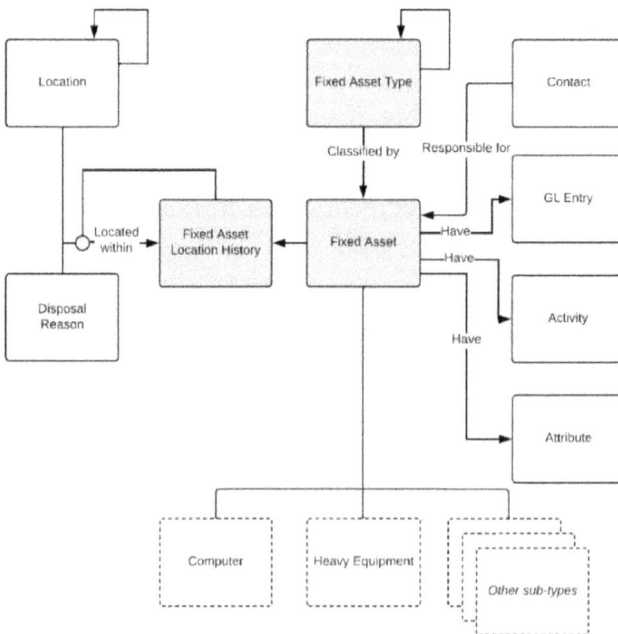

5.3.2.1   Fixed asset

At the core of the Fixed Asset model is an entity to capture information about fixed assets. It captures basic information found with most fixed assets, such as type, number, serial number, description, purchase date, disposal date, disposal reason, location, warranty period, and which contact is responsible for the asset (if any).

We can subtype Fixed Assets to capture more detailed information for other subtypes. Some examples of such assets are computers, vehicles, heavy equipment, and tools, to mention a few. To mitigate the propagation of many subtypes, the fixed asset system is often enhanced to track dynamic attributes determined by the fixed asset type.

5.3.2.2   Fixed asset location history

Fixed Asset Location History is a temporal entity that keeps track of the location of an asset. One of three location types locates an asset. Typically, assets are located within a location specified in the location hierarchy. An asset can also be located within another asset. For example, a computer peripheral exists within the main computer asset. Wherever the asset goes, the peripheral follows. The last location type is more nebulous. An asset can be disposed of for various reasons. Asset locations are mutually exclusive. An asset can never be in more than one location at any given time.

5.3.2.3   Fixed asset classification

The Fixed Asset Classification entity classifies Fixed Assets in the organization. It is a hierarchical breakdown that starts at high-level categories and breaks down into as many categories as required by the organization. This entity includes attributes such as description, notes, parent Fixed Asset Type (foreign key), and which subtype applies. For example, if the type of asset was a type of vehicle, then the subtype would refer to a vehicle subtype. The vehicle subtype contains attributes that describe a vehicle in more detail.

5.3.2.4   Location

The Location entity is referenced in the fixed asset model but it is also used in other models throughout the system like the personnel model. The Location entity is a hierarchical breakdown that starts at high-level locations and breaks down into as many locations as required by the organization. The Location entity includes attributes such as description, latitude/longitude, and parent location (foreign key).

5.3.2.5   Activity

Activities can be performed for assets. A maintenance activity is a good example. Assets can also perform activities. A good example is a construction company that charges assets and people to projects. The assets' activities have hours and billing rates, just like the activities performed by people.

5.3.2.6   Attribute

The generic Attributes entity tracks the attributes of assets.

5.3.2.7   Contact

Contacts are responsible for assets.

5.3.2.8   GL Entries

GL Entries in the financial system can be charged to assets. Examples include journal entries related to asset purchase, depreciation, expenses, and revenues.

5.3.3   User interface considerations

Users should be able to drill down to fixed assets from the following types of data.

- Drill down from any level in the location hierarchy.
- Drill down from any level in the asset classification hierarchy.
- Drill down from a contact to view the assets they are responsible for.

5.3.4   Data dictionary

Below are the data dictionary elements for the Fixed Asset Registry. Only the core tables appear.

Table Name	Column Name	Data-Type	Purpose
FixedAsset	ID	BigInt	3D primary key
FixedAsset	faStatusID	BigInt	Foreign key
FixedAsset	FixedAssetTypeID	BigInt	Foreign key

Table Name	Column Name	Data-Type	Purpose
FixedAsset	CostCenterID	BigInt	Foreign key
FixedAsset	Comments	Varchar	Data
FixedAsset	ContactID	Integer	Data
FixedAsset	DepreciationLife	Date	Data
FixedAsset	DepreciationSalvageValue	Decimal	Data
FixedAsset	Description	Varchar	Data
FixedAsset	ModelNumber	Varchar	Data
FixedAsset	Number	Varchar	Data
FixedAsset	PurchaseDate	Date	Data
FixedAsset	SerialNumber	Varchar	Data
FixedAsset	RowStatus	Char	System
FixedAsset	ChangeHistoryID	BigInt	Audit
Location-History	ID	BigInt	3D primary key
Location-History	ContactID	BigInt	Foreign key
Location-History	FixedAssetID	BigInt	Foreign key
Location-History	CommandID	BigInt	Foreign key
Location-History	DictionaryTableIDLocation	BigInt	Multilink
Location-History	RowIDLocation	BigInt	Multilink
Location-History	Details	Varchar	Data
Location-History	IsActive	Boolean	Data
Location-History	IsConfirmed	Boolean	Data
Location-History	TemporalStartDate	Date	Temporal
Location-History	TemporalEndDate	Date	Temporal
Location-History	RowStatus	Char	System
Location-History	ChangeHistoryID	BigInt	Audit
FixedAssetType	ID	BigInt	3D primary key
FixedAssetType	FixedAssetTypeIDParent	BigInt	Foreign key
FixedAssetType	GLAccountIDAccummulated-	BigInt	Foreign key

Table Name	Column Name	Data-Type	Purpose
	Depreciation		
FixedAssetType	GLAccountIDAsset	BigInt	Foreign key
FixedAssetType	GLAccountIDDepreciation-Expense	BigInt	Foreign key
FixedAssetType	DepreciationLife	Date	Data
FixedAssetType	DepreciationPercent	Integer	Data
FixedAssetType	Description	Varchar	Data
FixedAssetType	IsFixedAssetNumberUsed	Boolean	Data
FixedAssetType	IsUsedToClassifyRecords	Boolean	Data
FixedAssetType	ReplacementAmount	Decimal	Data
FixedAssetType	DisplaySequence	Integer	Data
FixedAssetType	Template	Varchar	Data
FixedAssetType	RowStatus	Char	System
FixedAssetType	ChangeHistoryID	BigInt	Audit

5.4   Activity registry

5.4.1   Overview

Some of the most important information for running an organization is knowing how resources spend their time. Yet, activity information fragments into many different systems with no ability to make connections. Some examples are:

- Sales funnel system that keeps track of sales activities.

- Customer Relationship Management system that keeps track of customer service activities.

- Contract management system that keeps track of activities for setting up and administering contracts.

- Fixed asset system that keeps track of fixed asset maintenance activities.

- Billing system that keeps track of billable activities.

- Absent time reporting system that keeps track of absences.

- Safety system that keeps track of safety incidents and the related investigations of follow-up.

- Training system which keeps track of the training received by individuals.

The activity module can track the detailed information for all of these systems and does so with a single activity registry that is simple yet powerful.

The key features of the activity module are:

- It tracks activities in various states (pending, planned, completed, etc.).

- It is flexible to track any type of activity performed by any resource (person, organization, or asset).

- It accommodates organizations that have regionalized databases.

- It provides a complete picture of all activities performed by or for a contact.

5.4.2 Data model design

The key to the Activities model is how the data is structured. The diagram below describes the core entities and how they are interrelated.

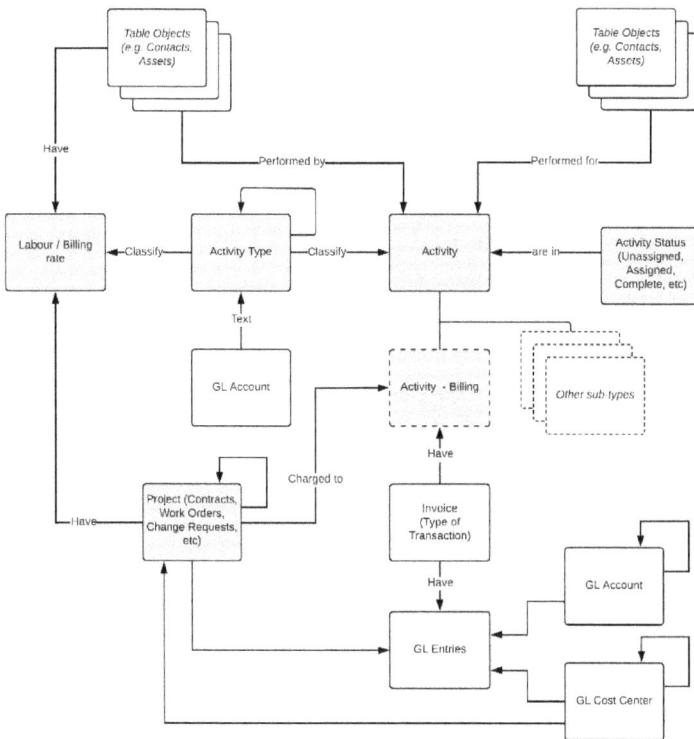

5.4.2.1   Activity

At the core of the Activity model is an entity to capture information about activities. An activity represents how an organization's resources spend their time. A user can drill down from any contact in the registry to view all activities performed for a contact. For example, if the contact is a prospect, the user would see all sales activities performed for the prospect.

A user can also drill down from a contact to see all activities performed by that contact. Fixed assets can also perform activities from the asset registry. For example, an asset may be used for eight hours on a particular date for a particular job.

Activities are typically performed for another contact but can also be performed for assets (such as with asset maintenance activities). In fact, an activity can be performed for any entity in the enterprise model that the organization requires (land parcel for land maintenance activities, oil and gas well for oil and gas well maintenance activities, etc.).

Which entity an activity gets connected to is controlled by parameters set on the Activity Type table. The Activity Type table also controls which subtypes get created.

The Activities entity has attributes such as activity type (foreign key), activity state (foreign key), performed for (foreign key), performed by (foreign key), description, unit of measure (foreign key), units, notes, and priority.

The activities can be refined into subtypes, and additional data can be tracked for each subtype. Some examples of this are:

- Sales activity – involves tracking details about the sales activity, such as what stage in the sales funnel it is at or what product it relates.

- Billing activity – involves tracking details related to the billing system, such as what contract it is related to or whether the activity is billable or non-billable.

- Asset maintenance activity – tracks additional details related to servicing a fixed asset.

- Workflow activity – tracks which step in the workflow process it is related to.

Activities can have more than one subtype, and organizations can add as many subtypes as they require to address their needs.

5.4.2.2   Activity type
The Activity Type entity classifies activities in the organization. It is a hierarchical breakdown that starts at high-level categories and breaks down into as many categories as required by the organization.

The Activity Type Scheme should represent a functional decomposition of the organization, with the purpose of the organization at the top and more detailed categories below.

The Activity Type entity includes attributes such as description, notes, parent activity type (foreign key), what entity the activity type is performed for (contacts, assets etc.), what entity the activity type is performed by (contact, asset, etc.), and what unit of measure should be used.

5.4.2.3 Activity states
The core activity states are:

- Completed – The activity has been completed and a completion date has been assigned.

- Planned – Planned activities have a start date assigned but are not completed.

- Pending – Pending activities have no start date and instead are assigned a priority.

These activity states can be used and augmented as required to meet the organization's needs.

5.4.2.4 Activity-billing
Activity-Billing is an example of a subtype of an activity record. This entity contains attributes that are specific for an activity record that is being billed. It contains attributes

such as the billing status, override of billing amounts, and a foreign key link to the invoice the activity was billed on.

5.4.2.5 Project

Projects is an example of an entity that can be set up for a project-based organization. The project is a hierarchical breakdown of projects, phases, and tasks. A project will have activities assigned to them. It can also have billing rates. When the project is billed, both expense and revenue journal entries can be related to the project.

5.4.2.6 Labor/billing rates

Billing and Expense Rates are two separate entities. Billing rates are billed for a given resource, and expense rates are for activity-based costing. The billing and expense rates can be related to a contact or asset. Billing and expense rates are temporal (i.e., they change over time).

Billing rates can be set up for a project. They can change based on the type of activity performed. Typically, billing rates are set up in a drill-down fashion where the billing system looks for the most specific billing rate (i.e., based on the resource, project, and type of activity performed). If it is not found, it looks for various combinations of resource, project, and type of activity based on the billing rules of the organization.

5.4.2.7 Invoice

Invoices is a type of transaction in the financial system. It is an example of a type of entity that connects to activities.

Monthly invoices are produced based on the billing rates and terms for the project. This causes journal entries to be created that connect to the project. Activities billed as a part of the project are connected to the invoice transaction.

5.4.3 Data dictionary

Below are the data dictionary elements for Activity Registry.

Table Name	Column Name	Data-Type	Purpose
Activity	ID	BigInt	3D primary key
Activity	actPriorityID	BigInt	Foreign key
Activity	actStatusID	BigInt	Foreign key
Activity	ActivityTypeID	BigInt	Foreign key
Activity	DictionaryTableID-PerformedBy	BigInt	Multilink
Activity	RowIDPerformedBy	BigInt	Multilink
Activity	DictionaryTableIDPerformedFor	BigInt	Multilink
Activity	RowIDPerformedFor	BigInt	Multilink
Activity	Comments	Varchar	Data
Activity	CompletionDate	Date	Data
Activity	Description	Varchar	Data
Activity	StartDate	DateTime	Data
Activity	TotalActual	Decimal	Data
Activity	RowStatus	Char	System
Activity	ChangeHistoryID	BigInt	Audit
Activity Type	ID	BigInt	3D primary key
Activity Type	CostUnitID	BigInt	Foreign key

Table Name	Column Name	Data-Type	Purpose
Activity Type	ActivityTypeIDParent	BigInt	Foreign key
Activity Type	GLAccountID	BigInt	Foreign key
Activity Type	MultilinkTableRuleID-PerformedBy	BigInt	Foreign key
Activity Type	MultilinkTableRuleID-PerformedFor	BigInt	Foreign key
Activity Type	Comments	Varchar	Data
Activity Type	Description	Varchar	Data
Activity Type	DisplaySequence	Integer	Data
Activity Type	RowStatus	Char	System
Activity Type	ChangeHistoryID	BigInt	Audit

5.4.4 User interface considerations

Users should be able to drill down to activities from any type of contact, asset, or other entity (e.g., oil and gas well, land). Activities may be performed for an entity or performed by an entity.

For billing systems, it is possible to create an activity-based costing module. An activity-based costing module analyzes finances by a different dimension: activities. Activity-based costing systems must be simple to administer and represent all revenues and expenses.

From a revenue perspective, all revenues for a project should be allocated to the activities. For fixed-price projects, revenues are allocated to each activity. The revenues are already associated with the activity for time and materials work.

The expense rates are a little more involved. A labor rate is established for each resource. On a regular frequency (e.g., quarterly), all charges for all activities based on the expense rates are calculated. Then, the expenses for that quarter are calculated. Next, a factor is applied that is multiplied by the labor rates so that the final total of labor rates for a quarter balances to the actual expenses.

The labor rate plus the factor provides the true expense of a resource, including expenses related to overheads such as office expenses. This process allows the analysis of profitability from two perspectives:

- Analyze profitability from a project perspective. This gives the true profitability of a project, including all overhead expenses.

- Analyze profitability from a resource perspective or any resource attribute (such as permanent or contract).

Having all activities consolidated in one place increases opportunities for features such as activity-based costing.

5.5 Human resources

5.5.1 Overview

The human resources module is a simple solution. The power of the module comes when organizations can roll-up information for positions and employee data from low levels to high levels for analysis.

5.5.2 Data model design

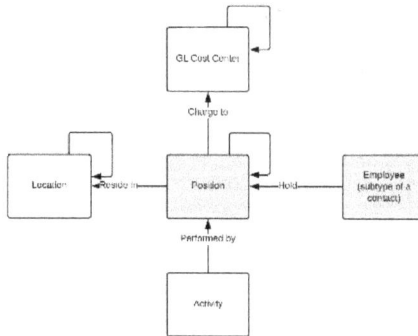

5.5.2.1 Position

Positions is a hierarchical breakdown of the positions that an employee can hold. Positions is temporal in that it changes over time. An employee can be associated with different positions over time. Each position will have a different temporal segment.

5.5.2.2 Employee

Employees are a subtype of Contacts. The employee subtype contains attributes about an employee regardless of their position (such as their commencement date).

5.5.2.3 Activity

Activities can be performed by a position or for a position without actually being performed for or by the individual.

5.5.2.4 Location

A Location is a hierarchical breakdown of the locations within an organization. A location can be a country, region, city, building, floor, or office. A position can reside in a location.

5.5.3 Data dictionary

Below are the data dictionary elements for the Human Resources Module. Only the core tables appear.

Table Name	Column Name	DataType	Purpose
Position	ID	BigInt	3D primary key
Position	LocationID	BigInt	Foreign key
Position	ContactIDEmployee	BigInt	Foreign key
Position	CostCenterID	BigInt	Foreign key
Position	GradeID	BigInt	Foreign key
Position	PositionClassificationID	BigInt	Foreign key
Position	PositionIDParent	BigInt	Foreign key
Position	PositionTypeID	BigInt	Foreign key
Position	CommencementDate	Date	Data
Position	Comments	Varchar	Data
Position	PositionNumber	Varchar	Data
Position	Salary	Decimal	Data
Position	DisplaySequence	Integer	Data
Position	TerminationDate	Date	Data
Position	WorkingTitle	Varchar	Data
Position	TemporalStartDate	Date	Temporal
Position	TemporalEndDate	Date	Temporal

Table Name	Column Name	DataType	Purpose
Position	RowStatus	Char	System
Position	ChangeHistoryID	BigInt	Audit

5.6 Financial module

5.6.1 Overview

The finance module benefits from all the design principles and architecture of the new paradigm. It benefits most from being able to:

- Create transactions in one system, accept them in another, and then have all the financial data connecting to all the right data, such as contracts, billing accounts, and projects.

- Connect financial data to temporal data so that finances can be analyzed by the data applicable at the time of the transaction.

- Access change history to easily see how parameters were changed that caused finances to be recalculated.

- Drill down from any entity in the database to see the related journal entries.

- Empower development teams to extend the financial module to track any type of transaction.

- Create a GL account structure by a central body, inherited by an industry body, and then inherited by an organization and extended as required. Creating GL account structures in this manner facilitates communication of financial records between all types of organizations.

This section discusses the data structures and elements to support the financial module. It also includes a description of the core utilities.

5.6.2 Data model design

The key to the financial model is how the data is structured. The diagram on the facing page describes the core entities and how they interrelate.

5.6.2.1 GL cost center

GL Cost Center is a recursive structure that identifies the cost/profit hierarchy used to classify journal entries to the appropriate cost/profit center. This structure is a recursive structure with the organization at the highest level and can be broken down to as many levels in the hierarchy as needed. Furthermore, the structure can be modified to add new cost/profit centers and add or eliminate levels within the hierarchy.

5.6.2.2 GL account

The GL Account recursive structure identifies the organization's hierarchical GL Account breakdown. The highest level in the account breakdown is the Balance Sheet entry. Beneath the Balance Sheet Entry are Asset, Liability, and Equity. The Net Income Account is beneath the Equity, while the Expense and Revenue Accounts are under Net Income.

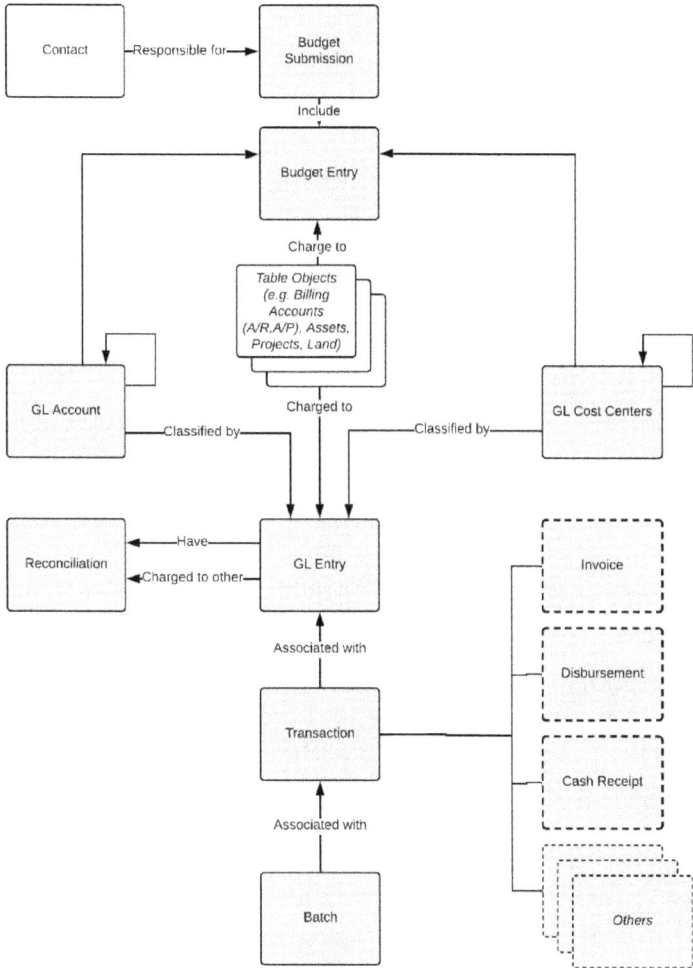

All the detailed accounts can be hierarchically broken down to as many levels as required. In addition, any given GL account can be further sub-classified by any object in the database per the user's choice. The most straightforward example is taking the Accounts Receivable Account and sub-classifying it by an A/R billing account. Other examples are sub-classify project-related expenses by project or asset-related expense/revenue/asset journal entries by asset.

5.6.2.3   GL Entry

Journal entries (GL entries) identify the amount to be charged to a GL Account and Cost Center. If the GL Account signals that it needs to be sub-classified by another object, the link to that object is identified. GL Entries also include a description, GL entry type, and a link to the associated transaction.

5.6.2.4   Transactions

The Transaction links all associated GL Entries together. It includes information such as the Transaction Date, Description, Reference Number, Status, and Batch ID (if the transaction is batch-oriented).

5.6.2.5   Batch

For transactions processed in batches, there is a batch record that links them together. The batch includes additional information such as a batch description, batch type, etc.

5.6.2.6   Budget entry

Budget Entries are similar to GL entries in that they represent what will be, rather than what was. Budget entries are charged to a GL Account and Cost Center. They can also connect to objects in the database. For example, a budget entry can connect to an oil and gas well or to a project.

Just like journal entries, there can be adjustments. For example, a budget entry could be set up for a project, and then adjusting budget entries are applied when the project scope changes.

5.6.2.7   Budget submission

A Budget Submission is like a transaction. There will be one or more budget entries associated with a budget submission. It will be assigned to a contact in the registry. Budget submissions can be in different statuses.

5.6.2.8   Table objects

A GL Entry or Budget Entry can be connected to any record within any table in the system. The linkage between table objects and journal entries/budget entries allows users to drill down from a table object (e.g., project, asset), view detailed entries, or produce a financial statement based on the table object.

5.6.2.9   Reconciliation

The Reconciliation entity allows for connections between payments, invoices, and adjustments. For example, when a customer submits payment for several invoices, reconciliation records are created to connect the payment to the invoices. In addition, the reconciliation entity allows for partial payments. For example, a customer submits payment and wants a specified amount applied to each invoice.

5.6.2.10 Subtyping of core entities

Batch, Transaction, and GL Entry tables can include additional data in subtype tables. For example, a transaction can include subtype data for A/P Invoice, A/R Invoice, Cash Receipt, and Disbursement.

5.6.3 Data dictionary

The data dictionary for the financial system only includes the core tables.

Table Name	Column Name	Data-Type	Purpose
GLAccount	ID	BigInt	3D primary key
GLAccount	GLAccountIDParent	BigInt	Foreign key
GLAccount	GLAccountTypeID	BigInt	Foreign key
GLAccount	MultilinkTableRuleID	BigInt	Foreign key
GLAccount	BankAccountNumber	Integer	Data
GLAccount	TopDownLevel	Integer	System
GLAccount	BottomUpLevel	Integer	System
GLAccount	Comments	Varchar	Data
GLAccount	Description	Varchar	Data
GLAccount	IsCollapseOnExport-Required	Boolean	Data

Table Name	Column Name	Data-Type	Purpose
GLAccount	IsUsedToClassifyRecords	Boolean	Data
GLAccount	QuickCode	Varchar	Data
GLAccount	ReferenceNumber	Varchar	Data
GLAccount	DisplaySequence	Integer	System
GLAccount	RowStatus	Char	System
GLAccount	ChangeHistoryID	BigInt	Audit
Batch	ID	BigInt	3D primary key
Batch	BatchStatusID	BigInt	Foreign key
Batch	BatchTypeID	BigInt	Foreign key
Batch	GLExportBatchID	BigInt	Foreign key
Batch	ApprovalDate	Date	Data
Batch	CreateDate	DateTime	Data
Batch	Description	Varchar	Data
Batch	FiscalYear	Integer	Data
Batch	HasBatchError	Boolean	Data
Batch	ChangeHistoryID	BigInt	Audit
Budget	ID	BigInt	3D primary key
Budget	GLAccountID	BigInt	Foreign key
Budget	CostCenterID	BigInt	Foreign key
Budget	Amount	Decimal	Data
Budget	Comments	Varchar	Data
Budget	BudgetDate	Date	Data
Budget	RollupAmount	Decimal	Data
Budget	RowStatus	Char	System
Budget	ChangeHistoryID	BigInt	Audit
CostCenter	ID	BigInt	3D primary key
CostCenter	CostCenterIDParent	BigInt	Foreign key
CostCenter	Comments	Varchar	Data

Table Name	Column Name	Data-Type	Purpose
CostCenter	Description	Varchar	Data
CostCenter	TopDownLevel	Integer	System
CostCenter	BottomUpLevel	Integer	System
CostCenter	IsUsedToClassifyRecords	Boolean	Data
CostCenter	ReferenceNumber	Varchar	Data
CostCenter	DisplaySequence	Integer	System
CostCenter	RowStatus	Char	System
CostCenter	ChangeHistoryID	BigInt	Audit
GLEntry	ID	BigInt	3D primary key
GLEntry	GLAccountID	BigInt	Foreign key
GLEntry	CostCenterID	BigInt	Foreign key
GLEntry	GLEntryTypeID	BigInt	Foreign key
GLEntry	TransactionID	BigInt	Foreign key
GLEntry	DictionaryTableID-ChargedTo	BigInt	Multilink
GLEntry	RowIDChargedTo	BigInt	Multilink
GLEntry	Amount	Decimal	Data
GLEntry	BankReconciliationDate	Date	Data
GLEntry	Comments	Varchar	Data
GLEntry	Description	Varchar	Data
GLEntry	ReconciliationBalance	Decimal	Data
GLEntry	ReferenceNumber	Varchar	Data
GLEntry	ReportingPeriodDate	Date	Data
GLEntry	RollupAmount	Decimal	Data
GLEntry	ChangeHistoryID	BigInt	Audit
Transaction	ID	BigInt	3D primary key
Transaction	BatchID	BigInt	Foreign key
Transaction	GLEntryIDMain	BigInt	Foreign key
Transaction	PostingStatusID	BigInt	Foreign key

Table Name	Column Name	Data-Type	Purpose
Transaction	TransactionIDReversed	BigInt	Foreign key
Transaction	TransactionTypeID	BigInt	Foreign key
Transaction	DictionaryTableIDSubType	BigInt	Foreign key
Transaction	CreateDate	DateTime	Data
Transaction	Description	Varchar	Data
Transaction	DueDate	Date	Data
Transaction	ReferenceNumber	Varchar	Data
Transaction	TransactionDate	Date	Data
Transaction	ChangeHistoryID	BigInt	Audit

5.6.4 Functional components

5.6.4.1 Introduction

This section discusses the main processes included in the core financial models.

5.6.4.2 Account balance rollup

The financial system allows users to select any level in an account hierarchy and then presents the numbers broken down by the cost center hierarchy. For example, the user can select a level in the cost center hierarchy and see a breakdown by GL account.

For example, the user could select a high-level account such as office expenses and then drill down and view office expenses by cost center. At the top of the cost center hierarchy would be the total office expenses for the organization. It will then be broken down hierarchically to the lowest level showing account balances at each level.

The user could then select a level in the cost center hierarchy and drill back to the GL account hierarchy to see a breakdown of the GL accounts beneath office expenses with account balances for the selected cost center.

An account balance rollup must be stored to provide this information. This function updates the account balance rollup whenever new journal entries post to the ledger. The function must deal with rolling numbers up the GL account hierarchy and GL cost center hierarchy. It must do this without looping because of the performance impact.

This function also rolls up budget entries and entries for reporting periods.

If the GL account hierarchy or the GL cost center hierarchy is reorganized, then the rollup function should be called to re-rollup the number based on the new hierarchy. However, adding new GL accounts or cost centers to the hierarchy does not necessitate a re-rollup.

5.6.4.3 Export

The export function creates journal entries for an external general ledger. For example, suppose the financial system was setup as a sub-ledger and an existing system was retained as the general ledger. In that case, this function will take the financial data and generate transactions for the general ledger.

This function will summarize journal entries based on rules in the chart of accounts. For example, a user may choose to summarize journal entries related to an account due to the volume of journal entries. If this option is selected, one summary GL Entry will be created for all the entries to that account for a given transaction date.

5.6.4.4   Auto reconcile

Reconciliation records are created to tie all invoices being paid to a payment. There is an algorithm to do this function automatically so that users do not have to do it manually.

5.6.4.5   Cash receipt

The cash receipt function can be called from the front end to pay invoices. It is set up to create all the financial records necessary for a cash receipt, such as journal entries and reconciliation records. In addition, it accommodates creating cash receipts for the payment of invoices that have barcodes using a simple one-click method.

If a cash receipt is using an online payment service, then the cash receipt function will be called from the front-end layer to create a pending cash receipt, and then the online payment service will be called. If the online payment service completes successfully, the cash receipt will be updated with details from the online payment service, and the status will be set to an approved status. In addition, the cash receipt will be flagged as deleted or physically deleted if the payment is not processed.

5.6.4.6 Batch approval

The batch approval process ensures the following of all business rules associated with the financial system. It also changes the transaction's status and calls the rollup function to rollup balances for reporting. This function is typically extended when new transaction types are added to a given system.

5.6.4.7 Integrity check

An integrity check function is included in the system, ensuring the following of the financial system's baseline rules. For example, if a property tax receivable billing account is created, then all journal entries charged to the billing account should also be charged to the property tax receivable account.

5.6.5 Generating automated billing functions

5.6.5.1 Introduction

One of the key development activities necessary for financial systems is creating routines to generate journal entries based on the data held in the database. The journal entries could be related to billing, penalty, or expense processes. This section discusses the steps necessary for analyzing these processes, then discusses the steps to create routines necessary to generate journal entries.

Automated billing functions must operate with high performance. Billing functions can result in hundreds of thousands of journal entries, so performance is imperative. As such, the methodology described in this section shows how to create a billing process while avoiding looping methods. A looping process involves processing records individually to generate journal entries. We should never use looping processes because of their impact on performance. Instead, we must use a series of insert, update, and select commands that deal with all records collectively. This section describes a methodology for analyzing requirements for billing processes and for generating journal entries without using any loops.

5.6.5.2 Analysis

You need a basic understanding of double entry accounting to work with users to define automated processes for generating journal entries. When analyzing these processes, ask these questions:

- What are the different types of journal entries you will be generating? For example, if it is a revenue process, you will have a journal entry for the receivable account, one or more revenue entries, and one or more tax entries.

- What is the algorithm for calculating each entry? You will need to understand where the data in the database is stored that is used as parameters for the algorithm.

- Do they need to subclassify any journal entries by entities in the database? For example, you will likely need to link the revenue entries to the related project record in a project billing system. In a property tax system, you may want to subclass revenue entries by the land parcel generating the tax revenue.

- How are adjustments handled? For example, if you generate journal entries for a revenue process based on parameters that change because of data updates, do you reverse the original transaction and re-post a new one, or do you create an adjusting journal entry?

- Is it possible to add new entries after running the original batch of journal entries? For example, if you generated a batch of journal entries for a billing process, would it be possible that something could get added that could cause generating a new invoice?

- What happens if a batch of journal entries is generated and then deleted before it is posted? Are there any updates or changes needed to parameter data? For example, in a time billing process, you may link the time records to the related invoice. If the invoice is deleted, you will need to detach the time records from the invoice so the time records can be re-billed.

- Is there data that needs to be locked from further updates after an invoice is approved? For example, in a time billing process, you may want to restrict users from updating those time records after a time record gets attached to an invoice and the invoice is approved.

- What warning/error conditions require checks? How does the system respond if a warning/error condition exists while generating journal entries? What about approving a batch that has warning/error conditions?

- If journal entries resulting from the generation process are exported to a general ledger, do you need to summarize those journal entries? For example, if a billing process generates hundreds of thousands of journal entries, it may be necessary to summarize those journal entries by GL account and date for some accounts. In this situation, if there were thousands of journal entries for a given GL account, only one journal entry with an aggregate amount would actually get created for the general ledger.

- Do the parameters change over time? Very likely, they will. That means you must set up all parameter data as temporal (time-sensitive). You will need to know what temporal resolution they are. It could be an annual temporal resolution meaning you only need to know what the temporal data looks like at the end of the year. Alternatively, temporal resolution could be daily or monthly.

- Do the users always generate everything based on the parameters, or do they sometimes only want to generate specific entries, such as all entries for a given contact?

5.6.5.3 Constraints

You will need to advise the users of the following constraints:

- It may seem like there is no need to allow for adjustments to occur because we do not expect the data that affects the journal entries to change. Inevitably though, if data can be entered, it can be entered wrong. As such, you always need to plan for an adjustment process that creates new records after the original generate process, that adjusts existing records due to changes or reversals of existing transactions.

- Users cannot create manual adjustments to circumvent the billing process or manually reverse invoices using journal entries. Instead, they must communicate these changes by changing the parameters to achieve the desired state.

5.6.5.4 Development

It is critically important that routines for generating journal entries be as performant as possible while maintaining an audit trail. To achieve these objectives, you will need to create parameter transaction records. The parameter transaction records are transaction records because there will be an initial transaction record and potentially adjustment or reversal records. We can total the transaction records together to give the final state for billing.

The parameter transaction records should include columns for any parameters directly affecting what gets billed. It should also include columns for data that affect what rate records get used. For example, if a province/state affects which tax rate is used, the province/state ID should be included.

It is also advisable to capture all possible drill-down paths to the parameter data for analysis. For example, if it was a time billing process, you may want to capture the client, project, resource performing the activity, GL account, cost center, activity ID, and batch ID.

In summary, you will capture all the parameters affecting billing and then compare them to previous billing cycles for the same period to see if anything changed. Specifically, the process for capturing billing processes is as follows:

1. **Setup financial batch.** Check to see if a batch already exists that is not approved. If so, you must delete the transactions, journal entries, and parameter transaction records associated with the batch. If a batch does not exist, create one.

2. **Collect parameter data.** In this process, you will collect all pertinent information according to the instructions above that affects the calculations in a temporary table. These entries should be collected according to invoices that are going to be generated.

3. **Determine adjustments.** Now that you know what to bill, you need to total up all the parameter entries for the same record to see what has been billed. You may find that the amount to be billed matches the amount previously billed (meaning nothing has changed), that the amount to be billed differs (meaning some parameter has changed), or that no previous amount was found indicating a new charge.

4. **Determine reversals.** Next, you need to compare your existing charges to your parameter file to see if they exist in your new parameter file. You need to set

up a reversal if they do not because whatever was previously charged no longer applies. At this point, you should be able to identify new charges, adjustments, and reversals. Now you need to post these entries to the database and proceed to generate journal entries based on the changes. The process will change slightly based on the requirements. For example, if the requirements state to create full reversal transactions (instead of adjusting existing transactions), then reversal transactions will need to be generated based on the cumulative charges.

5. **Generate transactions**. In this process, you will set up transaction records for any new invoices and adjustments. You can group your parameter transaction file by whatever uniquely makes up your invoices for this batch. That could be by project in a time billing system since you would likely not have two invoices in the same batch for the same project. You can use an output clause on the insert statement to write records to a transaction ID lookup table that contains the new transaction ID and identifying information for the invoice (like the project in the previous example). The lookup table will be used to lookup the transaction ID for billing records when creating journal entries.

6. **Generate revenue journal entries**. In this step, you will generate revenue journal entries based on your

parameters. You will group your parameters by the appropriate columns to create summary journal entries by GL account and GL cost center.

7. **Generate tax journal entries.** In this step, you will be analyzing the revenue journal entries and creating as many different types of tax journal entries based on the tax rules. It may be possible for entities to be tax exempt or services to be tax exempt.

8. **Generate receivable journal entries.** In this step, you will total the revenue and tax entries to determine the receivable entry. The revenue and tax journal entries will typically be negative (except for adjustments), and the receivable entries will typically be positive.

9. **Batch approval.** Once the batch has been reviewed, it will either be adjusted and regenerated or approved. When it is approved, the status of the transactions and batch will be set to Posted.

5.6.5.5   Summary

Creating a fast billing process with an appropriate audit trail is critically important to the success of a system. You should not use a loop process to generate invoices because of the performance impact. Instead, generate journal entries using an insert statement that adds all records at once. The process used for billing is very similar to penalty processes or for generating expense journal entries.

5.6.6   User interface considerations

5.6.6.1   GL account

The system includes a function for analyzing GL account balances. Users can browse a GL account hierarchy and view comparisons of actuals to either previous year values or budgets for a given time period.

We can base GL account amounts on the Fiscal Year amount or the Reporting Period amount. For example, if we pre-paid an expense for the year valued at $12,000 in January, we could set up journal entries for each month of the year with a different reporting period date. If we were analyzing by Fiscal Year amount, we would see a total of $12,000 in January and zero for all other months. If we were analyzing by Reporting Period, we would see $1,000 for each month of the year. If the GL account hierarchy contains many accounts and levels, we can call the function with parameters limiting the number of levels displayed. For example, if a user had to browse a GL account hierarchy with thousands of entries and many levels, it would be overwhelming to browse through all accounts at once. As such, the user could opt only to view the first three levels in the hierarchy and then drill down further from one of the entries to get more detail.

The GL account browse includes the following parameters:

- Reporting Date – Query date used for the date of the financial information to be displayed. The query date can be any month in any year. For example, if the query date is June, 20xx, then the current month balances and year-to-date values will be reflected for June 20xx.

- GL Cost Center – If passed, GL account balance information will be selected based on GL Cost Center. If it is null, it defaults to the highest level (root) cost center. For example, if Department A was passed as the GL Cost Center, all numbers reflected in the GL account hierarchy would be for Department A.

- Bottom-Up Level – If passed, the query results will be limited to hierarchy results where the GL account bottom-up value is less than or equal to the Bottom-Up Level. For example, when we look at the GL account hierarchy, we will see entries with no child entries below them. This is the lowest level of detail in the hierarchy, and it would have a bottom-up level of 1. The parent of entries with a bottom-up level of 1 have a bottom-up level of 2. This continues to the top of the hierarchy. This parameter allows the user to qualify which entries they want to see in the browse.

- Top-Down Level – If passed, the query results will be limited to hierarchy results where the GL account top-down value is less than or equal to the Top-Down Level. The Top-Down Level is the opposite of the Bottom-Up Level. It starts from the top of the hierarchy and works its way down. The highest-level entry in the hierarchy has a top-down level of 1. The GL accounts that are direct children to that entry have a top-down level of 2. This parameter filters the results based on the value passed. If a value of 3 was passed, then only the first three levels in the hierarchy would be displayed in the browse.

- Starting Position – If passed, the function will search for the first GL account where the description of the GL account is like the value passed. For example, if 'Office Expenses' was passed, the first account in the hierarchy with a description of 'Office Expenses' would be the first GL account displayed.

- Statement – Allowable values are Income Statement, or Balance Sheet.

- GL Account – If passed, the query results will traverse down from GL Account ID. It will default to the Balance Sheet account if it is not passed.

- Value Type – Allowable values are Fiscal Period Amount or Reporting Period Amount. For example, if Fiscal Period is selected, all values will be displayed based on the GL Entry amounts. If

Reporting Period is selected, then totals will be displayed based on the reporting period amount.

- Comparison Type – Allowable values are Previous Year or Budget Amount. For example, if Previous Year is selected, then the current month and year-to-date values will be compared to the Previous Year values. Otherwise, it will be compared to the budget amounts.

5.6.6.2 GL cost center

The system includes a function for analyzing cost center balances. Users can browse a cost center hierarchy and view comparisons of budgets to actuals for a given time period. If the cost center hierarchy contains many cost centers and levels, the function can be called with parameters limiting the number of levels displayed.

The Cost Center Browse includes the following parameters:

- Reporting Date – Query date used for the date of the financial information to be displayed.

- GL Account – If passed, GL Account Balance information will be selected based on GL Account. If null is passed, then the GL Account defaults to Income Statement.

- Bottom-Up Level – If passed, the query results will be limited to hierarchy results where the Cost Center bottom-up value is less than or equal to the Bottom-Up Level.

- Top-Down Level – If passed, the query results will be limited to hierarchy results where the Cost Center top-down value is less than or equal to the Top-Down Level.

- Starting Position – If passed, the query results will traverse down from the first Cost Center where the description is, such as Starting Position.

- Cost Center – If passed, the query results will traverse down from Cost Center. If it is not passed, it will default to the Balance Sheet Cost Center.

- Value Type – Allowable values are Fiscal Period Amount or Reporting Period Amount.

- Comparison Type – Allowable values are Previous Year or Budget Amount.

5.6.6.3 GL account cost center history

This function summarizes account balance history based on the GL account and cost center.

The function includes the following parameters:

- Reporting Date – Query date used for the date of the financial information to be displayed. Defaults to the year-end specified in the financial setup.

- Cost Center – Can be any level in the Cost Center hierarchy. Defaults to the highest level in the cost center hierarchy.

- Account – Can be any level in the GL Account hierarchy. If it is null and the statement is an income statement, then it defaults to the Net Income Account. If the statement is a balance sheet, then it defaults to the Balance Sheet Account.

- Period – Month, Annual.

- Value Type – Allowable values are Fiscal Period Amount or Reporting Period Amount.

- Comparison Type – Allowable values are Previous Year or Budget Amount.

- Rows – Number of rows to return.

- Statement – Allowable values are Income Statement or Balance Sheet.

5.6.6.4   Biggest contributor

This function allows users to narrow down the main contributing factor that caused a difference between periods.

The function includes the following parameters:

- Reporting Date – Query date used for the date of the financial information to be displayed.

- Account – If passed, the query results will traverse down from GL account. It will default to the Income Statement account if it is not passed.

- Cost Center – If passed, GL Account Balance information will be selected based on Cost Center. If null is passed, the Cost Center defaults to the highest level (root) cost center.

- Value Type – Allowable values are Fiscal Period Amount or Reporting Period Amount.

- Period – Month Amount or Annual Amount.

- Statement Type – Allowable values are Income Statement or Balance Sheet.

- All – If true, then the report will analyze all child records. Otherwise, it will just analyze at the current GL account and cost center level.

5.6.6.5   Odd month

This function checks for situations where we see odd months. An odd month is where we normally see a recurring pattern of a number, but one month in the middle has a different value.

The function includes the following parameters:

- Start Month – Starting month to check. Defaults to the beginning of the fiscal year.

- End Month – Ending month to check. Defaults to the end of the fiscal year.

- Account – If passed, the query results will traverse down from GL account. It will default to the Income Statement account if it is not passed.

- Cost Center – If passed, GL account balance information will be selected based on Cost Center. If null is passed, then the Cost Center defaults to the highest level (root) cost center.

- Rows – Number of rows to return. Defaults to 100.

- Value Type – Allowable values are Fiscal Period Amount or Reporting Period Amount.

- Min Percentage – Minimum percentage changes to look for.

- Minimum Amount – Minimum amount to check for.

5.6.6.6 *Missing period*

This function checks for situations where we see a charge for several months followed by a missed charge followed by more charges. The intent is to identify a missed expense or revenue.

The function includes the following parameters:

- Start Month – Starting month to check. Defaults to the beginning of the fiscal year.

- End Month – Ending month to check. Defaults to end of fiscal year.

- GL Account – If passed, the query results will traverse down from GL account. It will default to the Income Statement account if it is not passed.

- Cost Center – If passed, GL account balance information will be selected based on cost center. If null is passed, the cost center defaults to the highest level (root) cost center.

- Rows – Number of rows to return. Defaults to 100.

- Value Type – Allowable values are Fiscal Period Amount or Reporting Period Amount.

- Minimum Amount – Minimum amount to check for.

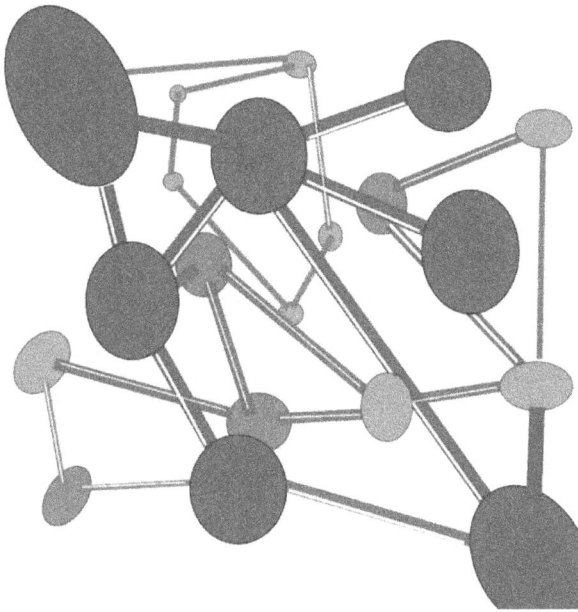

6 Application Framework

6.1 Overview

The application framework controls the user interface. The more sophisticated the framework, the more features users will be able to enjoy. It also controls the security system. The better the application framework, the more secure the system. The application framework also impacts the speed of developing new systems and their ease of maintenance. In the old paradigm, frameworks are being redesigned and developed with every system. That means if an organization uses a hundred different systems (package or custom), development teams have recreated the application framework many times.

In the new paradigm, a few organizations will specialize in creating application frameworks in a standardized manner. This standardization will allow organizations to change application frameworks just like they can switch web browsers.

This section discusses the mandatory and desirable features within an application framework. We researched many frameworks and consolidated the best features into an ideal application framework.

6.2 User authentication

The framework will provide a method for users to sign in and authenticate themselves. The other requirements of the user authentication engine from a framework perspective are as follows:

- Ability to use other authentication services.

- Ability to set and enforce password policies.

- Ability to time out sessions.

- Ability to change passwords.

- Ability to track authentication attempts in the change history.

6.3 Menu Options

6.3.1 Introduction

This section of framework features discusses features built into the framework for users to initiate actions for menus. These features aim to help users find what they need to access in a methodical manner, while providing fast and efficient ways to initiate menu options.

6.3.2 Hierarchical access to menus

The framework will need to provide hierarchical access to menus so a user can drill down from high-level subjects and eventually get to the menu option of interest. In large systems, thousands of menu options can exist, making this task complex. The menu options may appear on a page, in a drop-down menu, or in any other method that allows users to drill down and select the right option.

6.3.3 Provide fast and efficient ways of accessing menu options

The framework should provide fast and efficient methods of finding menu options, such as:

- Entering a menu number/name directly.

- Browsing insert menu options and selecting one to execute (e.g., insert contact, insert invoice, etc.).

- Browsing data maintenance options and selecting one to execute (e.g., maintain contacts, maintain assets).

- Using hotkeys to access frequently used menu options.

- Presenting users with their previously selected menu options so that the user can quickly select menu options of interest.

- Allowing users to create a favorites list of menu options.

6.3.4 Multi-lingual captions, tool tips, help text

The framework will present the captions, hover text, and help text from the command system based on the user's language preferences.

6.3.5 Security

Users will only see the menu options they are permitted to view based on their user privileges.

6.4 Search/browse data

Some menu options will cause creating an action tab in the form of a search/browse tab. Typically, a search form will qualify the results set coming back from the database. However, in some cases, the initial search tab is not required. Below is a description of the search and browse capabilities.

6.4.1 Search form

- The search form limits the data retrieved from the database which appears in the browse form.

- Parameters stored in the database determine the search form's construction.

- The search form fields will be in the form of text boxes, single pick lists, multi-pick lists, or checkboxes.

- The user's language preferences will determine the captions extracted from the database.

- The search forms for temporal data should allow the user to override the default query date for the current search form.

6.4.2 Browse form

The browse form presents a grid with the data returned from the database based on selected search form results. The user can toggle between the search and browse forms to alter the search results they are viewing. The framework should provide users with the following features from a browse form.

6.4.2.1   Creation of browse form

The browse form should be fully constructed based on information from the database. This includes:

- Presenting the columns in the appropriate sequence, which is either based on the default or the user's previous preferences.

- Presenting column headings based on the user's language preferences.

- Presenting columns with the appropriate widths based on the default or the user's preferences.

- Presenting the grid in the appropriate sort order.

- Presenting the user with all the menu options that are available for the browse (e.g., add, edit, delete, drill down, export, etc.).

The browse form will need to retrieve its data from a programmatically generated view based on browse form parameters. Developers will have the option of overriding this view as required.

6.4.2.2   Filtering data in the grid

The browse form should support filtering based on one or more columns. The filter should include options such as equals to, contained in, not contained in, etc.

6.4.2.3   Personalize the grid

The browse should allow users to personalize grids in the following manner:

- Click on columns to change sort order.

- Rearrange the sequence of columns in the grid and hide/unhide columns.

- Pin columns to the right or the left.

- Pin rows to the top or the bottom.

- Create rules for conditional formatting of columns (e.g., highlight cells/rows with a particular font color or background color).

6.4.2.4   Paging feature

The browse form should support paging. Paging only returns the first page of data on the initial query but allows a user to navigate through results and navigate to the first and last page of data.

6.4.2.5   Export data

The framework will support exporting to a spreadsheet, PDF, or document. The user should be able to select all rows or rows for export.

6.4.2.6   Take actions on rows

The browse form should provide various methods for taking actions based on the data in the grid, which in turn is based on their security privileges. These methods include:

- Using the menu bar to select a menu option to execute for the selected record(s).

- Using short-cut keys to access menu options directly.

- Right-clicking on a row and seeing a context menu appear, which shows all options available for the current row.

- Clicking on a row and having either a view or edit form open.

- Clicking on a hyperlink foreign key value in the grid and opening either a view or edit form.

- Supporting the ability to edit multiple records.

6.4.2.7   View related data (drill down)

One of the common actions on the grid is to support the ability to view related drill downs. For example, a user can right-click on a row and a context menu will appear, showing all the drill-down options. One of the more popular options for the drill down will be to view the change history for the selected record.

6.4.2.8 Take actions on multiple records at one time

The browse form should allow the user to select multiple records and take action. An example is multi-edits, where a user can select multiple rows and make an update to a specific column. The security system will control the ability to perform multi-edits. The change history log tracks updates.

6.4.2.9 Mail merge engine

The browse form should support a connection to the mail merge engine for any forms with a link to the contact. The mail merge engine allows a user to process all rows or selected rows in the browse list. The user can then either create a new mail merge document or select an existing document.

The mail merge engine will take contents from the browse columns and insert them into the mail merge document as required.

For more information on the mail merge engine, refer to the mail merge administration section later in this chapter.

6.4.2.10 Edit data directly in the grid

The browse form should support data editing directly in the grid for both master and detail data. It will process the updates according to business rules from the database and will capture updates in the change history log. The ability to edit will be controlled by whether a user can edit within the grid or not.

6.4.2.11 Master data with detail tabs

The browse form should support browsing of child data for records if they exist. For example, if we are browsing for data about projects, we can see child tabs at the bottom of the page, such as activities performed for the project, resources assigned to the project, etc. Furthermore, the user can click from one child tab to the next to see different child records.

6.4.2.12 Advanced features of the grid

The browse form may include advanced features for users, such as:

- Creating a pivot table and/or graph directly from the grid.

- Viewing the grid result on a map if latitude/longitude coordinates are available.

- Performing a mail merge from the grid if the grid contains information for a contact.

6.4.2.13 Save search criteria and formatting to a favorites menu

The framework should allow users to save search criteria and formatting to a favorites list so they can access it later.

6.4.2.14 Manage formatting

The framework will allow system administrators to create a new default format and delete existing ones for users (if removing a column from the column list, for example). It also should allow users to change their formatting to the default format.

6.5 Edit form

The framework needs to provide the ability to edit data in a form mode. The form can have multiple dynamic tabs based on a user's security setting and the nature of the edited record. The form must be used in Add, Edit, Delete, and View modes.

New edit forms will be opened with a caption based on the command executed plus context information (e.g., name of contact). The form should include some type of indicator (e.g., *) to indicate that the record needs to be saved.

The data on the edit form should not be written to the database until the user presses a save button. This includes inserting, updating, and deleting child data in tabs. A data maintenance utility that is a function within the database accomplishes this task. The front-end layer will call the data maintenance utility in read mode, which will return an object in a document format that includes data for the main entity plus all the child entities.

The edit form will modify this data object as it requires. This could be modifying the main entity and/or adding, editing, or deleting any of the records for child entities. When the user presses the save button, the front-end layer will call the data maintenance utility in update mode. This will cause it to compare the revised data object with the database and make all the necessary inserts, updates, and deletes within a transaction.

6.5.1 Creation of edit form

We construct the edit form primarily from information held in the database. This includes:

- Placing the controls in the right location on the form with the appropriate caption based on the user's language preferences. Examples of controls are tabs, grids, and various types of column controls (text, date, single pick list, multi-pick list, radio control). In addition, the edit form should support custom controls to support specialized needs.

- All business rules for processing, navigating, and validating data columns should be retrieved from the database with the ability to have custom rules.

- The framework can create forms dynamically from the database, precompile forms to improve performance, or a combination thereof (compile on first-time use).

- The framework should check row and column level security and act appropriately. Additionally, the system should check for rules of governance on the record and ensure that the current system has the authority to update or delete the record.

6.5.2 Types of controls

The edit form could include the following controls:

- Date control allows a user to enter a date. Other features of a date control include popping up a calendar and allowing the user to navigate the calendar easily. Also, a user should be able to easily select the current date, increase/decrease a day at a time, or increase/decrease by a certain number of days (e.g., +/- 10).

- Time control allows the user to enter a time value.

- Date/time control allows a user to enter a date/time value.

- Text control allows a user to enter a text value.

- Note control allows a user to enter a note value. Advanced features of a note control will include the ability to format text, ranging from simple formatting up to sophisticated formatting, such as word processing packages.

- Radio control allows a user to enter a bit value.

- Numeric control allows users to enter integers and decimal values. Including a calculator in the control will be desirable.

- Single pick list allows users to select a value from a list of foreign key values. Features of the single pick list are:

  o Will allow a search value to be entered in the text box where the search results adjust accordingly.
  o Will accommodate cached and non-cached values (for small and large lists).
  o Will filter records flagged as inactive but allow the filter for inactive records to be turned off so that records can be selected.
  o Will filter based on the query date for temporal records.
  o Will return the translation for the foreign key, which must default to the translation stored in the data dictionary. The translation can be overridden on a particular form as required.
  o Should allow the user to pop up the complete maintenance list for the table and perform any permitted action, including adding, editing, deleting, and drilling down related data.

- Multi pick list allows a user to select multiple values and returns a comma-delimited list of all values selected. The multi-pick will have all the same features as the single pick list, except for allowing multiple values to be selected.

- Multimedia control allows a user to maintain any type of multimedia (photo, movie, sound clip, etc.).

6.5.3 Defaulting of values

When values are added to a form, the user should have the ability to specify a default value based on the following list:

- Default the value based on a record currently selected.

- Default the value based on a value set from the browse list. For example, if the browse list is a list of activities performed by a staff member and the user selects 'Performed by', it will default to the staff member in the browse list.

- Default based on a value specified by the user. The user can specify a default value for any form in this case.

- Default the value based on a fixed value.

6.5.4 Validation

The form uses validation rules retrieved from the database. Validation can be performed on the client, server, or both sides — for each field, as it is processed, and for all fields on all tabs when the record is saved.

- Validation will use multi-lingual messages stored in a message table.

- Validation will highlight all fields on all tabs where an issue exists. Likewise, it will provide a list of all errors and warning conditions.

- Validation rules will apply to both form edits and browse edits.

6.5.5 Governance

We check governance rules for all records before editing them. The general rule for governance is that if a system creates a record, it can update or delete it, provided that governance has not been granted to another system.

If a user attempts to update a record that the system does not have the governance rights to, the system will warn them. Users can be granted the authority to update a record not governed by the system they use. Transferring governance between systems is in place, so we always know which system owns the gold version of that record.

Two different systems can have update capabilities to the same record at the same time, but for two different temporal ranges that do not overlap.

6.5.6 Concurrent updates

The framework should check for an update to a record since the last time a user opened it for updating. For example, if user A opened a record to update it and User B opened the same record, made updates, and saved it, user A should be warned that a concurrent update had occurred and discard the updates.

6.5.7 Temporal access

The user interface will show a user if multiple temporal versions of a record exist. It will then allow the user to switch between those temporal versions. Also, if the user has the necessary authority, they can insert a new temporal segment anywhere in the temporal range, eliminate a temporal record, or edit any temporal record. Change history tracks all changes to temporal records.

6.5.8 Hyperlinks

A user should be able to send the hyperlink for a record to another user, and that user, in turn, should be able to click on it and view/edit the record, provided they have the requisite permissions. For example, if a user was sending an email to another user about a member, it would be desirable if they could copy/paste a hyperlink into the email for the member. Then, when the user receives the email, they should be able to click on the hyperlink and have the member form open with the appropriate member record, providing the user is authenticated and has the appropriate privileges.

6.5.9 Pre-/post-processing

The framework should allow for executing pre- and post-processing rules for any form. In the standard post-processing logic, validations for all columns are processed, and the data is saved to the database.

6.5.10 Save/close features

The framework may provide the following advanced features for forms:

- Add Next, which allows a user to save the current record and open a form for a new record all with one action.

- Edit Next, which saves and closes the current form and opens the next record in the browse form all with one action.

- Shortcut keys to perform all actions on the form (Save and Close, Add Next, Edit Next, etc.).

6.6 Searching For data

6.6.1 Search engine style search

The Search Engine Style Search will allow users to enter a value and return all browse lists where that value was located in both master and detail records. For example, a user can enter 'ABC Corp' and see the ABC Corp contact record, contracts with ABC Corp, financial records for ABC Corp, etc. The user can qualify the search by subject categories such as finance or financial journal entries. The user's sign-in capabilities will limit the search results. Other features of the search capability will be:

- Qualification of the search based on equals, contained in, begins with, etc.

- Qualification based on the source of the column to a column in a table (such as contact name).

- Limiting search results to a specified number of rows.

- All capabilities of the browse will be available to the user to perform actions (add, edit, delete, drill down, etc.).

6.6.2 Tag records

Tag records allow users to tag any record in the system with a # tag value and then search and retrieve records in a similar method to the Search Engine Style Search. Public and private # tag values will be available to users when flagging and searching for values.

6.7 Temporal capabilities

6.7.1 Query date maintenance

The query date controls the temporal data being returned to a user. Authorized users can backdate the temporal date to any previous date. This will cause all temporal data to appear as of that date. It will also cause the automatic temporal capability to set up new temporal records with the default start date as required.

6.7.2 Temporal resolution

A default temporal resolution is set for a given system but can be overridden on a table-by-table basis. Temporal data is captured based on different time resolutions. For example, the resolution may be a fiscal year in a government setting. It may be to the day for a health and benefits system and to the second in an oil and gas system. If the temporal resolution was a day and the same temporal record was updated twice on the same day, the second update will merely update the existing record and not cause a new record to be created. All changes to temporal records are tracked in the change history.

6.8 Reporting services

The framework will provide a connection to a report development tool. The system should be able to invoke reports from within the menu system based on security privileges. Users should be able to create new reports and embed them in the menu systems for both public and private reports. Report parameters should be stored in the database just as browse form and edit form parameters are stored. The report parameters will tie into the data dictionary for the system.

6.9 Change history

The change history parameters can be modified to change which commands, tables, and columns change history tracks. The user should be able to browse change history from the following perspectives:

- View the change history for a record (e.g., drill down and see the change history for a particular contact record).

- View the change history that resulted from a particular menu option.

- View the change history that resulted from a particular user or their department.

- View all changes to a particular column and view the associated change history transaction.

6.10 Workflow processes

The framework should include the ability to design and update workflow processes. Other features the workflow module should support are as follows:

- Support the creation of workflow processes graphically.

- Provide actions, decision points, and flow controls (looping) that can be inserted into a workflow process. Select these items from the rules engine.

- Able to connect any browse or edit forms into the workflow process.

- Able to work forward and backward through the workflow process.

- Able to suspend a workflow process, in which case apply no updates to the database.

- Able to spawn other workflow processes.

- Presents the user with a list of all workflow processes assigned to complete and provides them with a history of completed and canceled workflow processes.

- Provides statistics to management for counts and duration times.

6.11 Dashboards

The user can personalize the dashboard. The requirements of the dashboard are to allow the user to:

- Add, edit, and delete widgets on their dashboard and size them accordingly.

- Refresh content as required.

6.12 Soft deletes

The 3D ES framework has capabilities for soft deleting data. A soft delete causes a record to no longer be visible on a selection list, but the record continues to exist to maintain referential integrity. For example, a contact may cease to exist and need to be eliminated from the registry so it will not appear in selection lists throughout the application. We cannot just delete the contact record because child data (such as financial transactions) reference the contact.

As such, we set the row status on the contact's record to 'd', which will cause the contact record to no longer appear in any selection lists. However, the contact's data will still be visible if there are foreign key references to that contact.

Soft deletes are also possible with temporal data. Any segment within a temporal series can be soft deleted. That could be the first segment in the series, a middle one, or the last one. Search forms should be able to include soft deleted records if the user chooses to see them. Browse forms should highlight soft deleted records differently than normal ones.

6.13 Duplicate detection and merging

One issue to address in 3D ESs is helping users identify if a record already exists before adding a new one. Even with these capabilities, duplicate records get added. Therefore, maintenance capabilities are required to identify potential duplicates and eliminate them. The framework should include the following built-in capabilities to aid in this task:

- Use information from the data dictionary to change foreign keys from the old to the new record.

- Use information from the data dictionary to identify potential duplicates.

6.14 Offline processing

Offline processing allows tasks to be pushed to the background, so they don't affect online processing. The framework should support the following requirements for offline processing:

- Queues and the ability for administrators to create as many queues as required.

- Job prioritization in the queue.

- User notification when offline jobs complete.

- Job cancelation in the queue.

6.15 Rules engine

The rules engine maintains rules in the database that connect to entities in the enterprise database. For example, rules exist to aid in adjudicating claims in a Health and Benefits administration system. The rules connect to a health plan in the system so that the rules only execute for that particular health plan. An example of rules in an oil and gas scenario is rules to distribute costs to oil and gas wells based on contract terms. Rules are temporal in that they can change over time and, as such, execute relative to a query date.

The framework should support the following requirements for rules engines:

- A user-friendly dialect for advanced users to detect conditions and take action.

- The ability to connect to any object in the database.

- The ability to capture syntax errors in the error handling system.

6.16 Error processing

The framework will provide central error handling. The requirements of the central error handling are:

- Provide informative messages to the user that they have encountered an error and that their work may not complete as expected.

- Log the error in a central location.

- Include escalation capabilities for notifying system staff.

- Include the ability to clear the error log.

6.17 Creating/maintaining automation parameters

The framework will support an entire engine for creating and maintaining new systems. The maintenance engine will have the following capabilities:

- Maintain the following system parameters and store them in system tables:
  o Commands/menu options
  o Search/browse/edit form parameters
  o Data dictionary
  o Security groups
  o Rules

- ○ Dashboard widgets
- ○ Workflow processes
- ○ Messages
- ○ Reports
- ○ User preferences

- Support multiple languages.

- Support governance controls.

- Support versioning.

- Automate parameters between systems.

- Allow custom forms/controls to be created and blended into the system.

- Allow an organization to brand the look and feel of the application with its own logo, colors, and fonts.

6.18 Interface to the SQL database

Developers use a language like Javascript or NODE.js for the initial version of the front-end framework. Some frameworks include plugins for interfacing to any type of database engine, whether a SQL or NoSQL database. Such a plugin can quickly switch from one database to another without having to update front-end code.

While this might seem attractive, this is the lowest common denominator for features. There is a substantial difference in features between SQL and NoSQL databases. As a result, it will be like using a SQL database as if it was a key-value pair database. The application front-end will connect directly to the database using a wrapper approach instead of utilities. Database wrappers centralize all logic for interacting with a database, so switching from one database to another is simple. The goal of these wrappers is to fully leverage the capabilities of a given database with the thinnest interface possible, thereby maximizing performance.

6.19 Deployment

One of the key issues the new paradigm will need to deal with is deployment. The challenge with deployment in the old paradigm is that it can be extremely complex to deploy an entire application all at once. This creates the risk that some application components will fail when deploying the entire application. Then the support team is left to fix the deployment quickly or roll it back, which can be extremely complex.

In the new paradigm, there will be less need for full deployments of the application. We can make substantial changes to the system without rebuilding and redeploying the system. For example, we can add a new browse with edit form, including all the supporting commands like drill down, and no build would be required. A script would be created and tested in development, then moved to the test environments and finally to production without rebuilding the system. We can even track change history on the script and undo it quickly if there is an issue.

A full deployment would be necessary only when the application framework (which leverages source code) changes.

To further alleviate the deployment issues, we can use a microservices architecture to create the application framework. To have microservices blend well with 3D ES, microservices will need to utilize stored procedures for performing transactions (so we eliminate ACID-compliance issues) and leverage views to access data (so we eliminate the complexities with keeping duplicated data in sync between microservices).

This is not to say that the 3D ES database would store the entire enterprise database. There could be major components of the system that leverage NoSQL databases.

6.20 Data model design

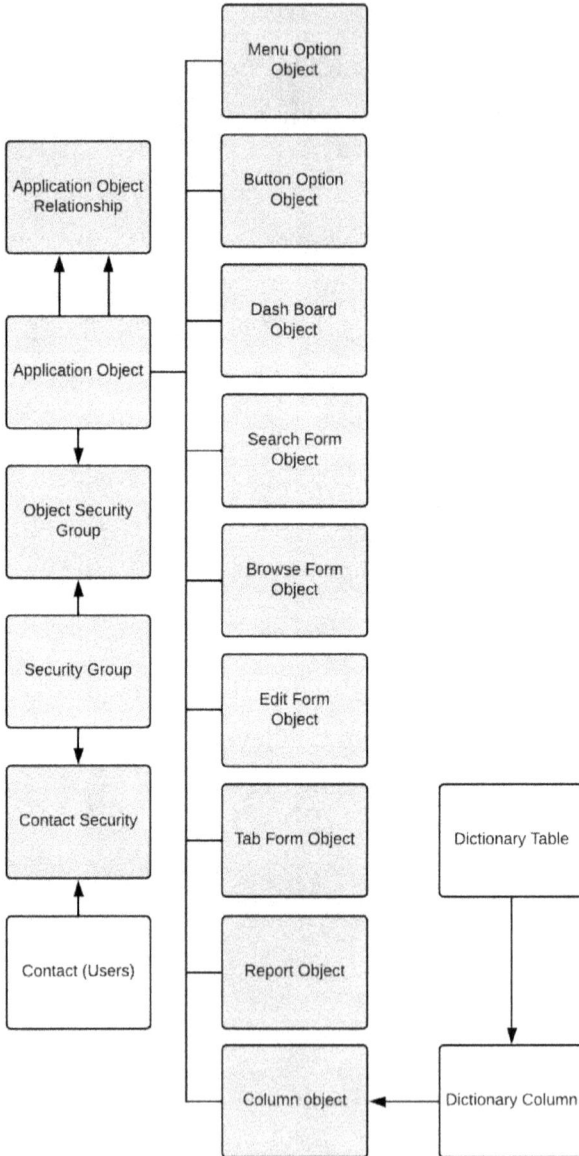

6.20.1 Application object

This represents the key objects to use in creating an application. The application object has the following subtypes:

- Menu Option Object – menu options that start at high levels, such as contact maintenance and work, down to menu options, such as 'Maintain Contact'.

- Button Option Object – buttons that appear on forms. For example, the address tab on the contact form will have buttons for adding, updating, and deleting addresses for a contact.

- Dashboard Object – objects that appear on a dashboard.

- Search Form Object – search criteria for filtering records on a browse list.

- Browse Form Object – objects that allow users to browse data.

- Edit Form Object – objects that allow editing of data. Columns can be placed directly on edit forms or organized within tabs.

- Tab Form Object – objects that exist on an edit form.

- Report Object – objects for reporting.

- Column object – objects that relate to a specific column.

6.20.2 Application object relationship

This entity contains information about how the objects relate to one another. There is a many-to-many relationship between objects. For example, a tab object has many column objects that are a child to it, but at the same time, a tab object can exist on many edit forms, thereby having many parents.

6.20.3 Security group

A security group is defined as grouping many objects together for security.

6.20.4 Object security group

An object is placed into one or more security groups.

6.20.5 Contact security

A contact is granted access to one or more security groups.

6.21 Summary

Considering all the functionalities to implement in a framework, you will realize the massive duplication of effort we see in our old paradigm. User interfaces and the application frameworks that support them are being designed and built for almost every system created.

In the new paradigm, we build frameworks a few times rather than once per system. We base frameworks on standardized core parameters stored in the database. Some frameworks will extend the parameters to support additional functionality.

Frameworks will be more powerful than ever because organizations will specialize in creating frameworks rather than every team dedicating time and money to build their own. Some suppliers of frameworks will specialize in creating light, simplistic interfaces that are inexpensive and simple to implement. In contrast, others will create industrial strength frameworks with robust features for users. The new paradigm benefits application frameworks because of its efficiencies for IT professionals and the expense it could save organizations.

7 Methodology for Architecting a 3D ES

7.1 Creating the vision

7.1.1 Building the case

During the early days of the new paradigm, it will take a lot of effort to make the change. It will likely start with you reading this book and applying the methodology to your organization. Eventually, it will make its way up the line to someone with authority to set aside a small budget to get started with a vision and plan.

Next, produce the business case. It will include information from this book aimed at executives, such as why the current approach to ESs is failing us and how we can make improvements. You will supplement the information with specifics from your organization, such as the number of systems you have and how your IT budgets have changed over time. The business case will likely recommend an incremental approach to solve the integration problem, where the organization can suspend the process at any stage and still receive value. For example:

1. Create an enterprise data dictionary by reverse engineering one system at a time.

2. Classify the data to see the duplication across subject areas and all the data captured about a given subject.

3. Use the data dictionary to generate views and consolidate data into a data warehouse.

4. Produce registry systems one by one to manage all the data for a given subject area and then build interfaces to the existing systems.

5. Begin creating 3D ESs by locality that tie into the registry systems. And during the process, create common functionality to share among 3D ESs.

7.1.2 Developing the vision

Next, describe in more detail how the 3D ESs in the organization will interconnect. The 3D ES website will provide information based on industry-specific vision templates. The vision statement will describe the functional scope of the 3D ESs, how master data will be shared between them, how to roll up data for reporting, and the migration plan for moving from the existing or legacy systems to 3D ESs.

7.1.3 Cost-benefit analysis

The cost-benefit analysis will be a critical task. It will involve delving into the problems with the old paradigm approach and the costs to the organization. Specifically, it will look at the IT costs associated with maintenance, licensing, and data warehouse/reporting. The IT costs will also need to consider the cost of replacing systems due to outdated technology or the cost of implementing a large vendor-specific ES.

Next, you will look at the cost to the organization for having to use systems that are not integrated. Subject matter experts will need to provide information on challenges they face due to non-integrated systems. It may be hard for them to imagine a world where data is not keyed from one system to the next and then reconciled. It may help to share the vision of how a 3D ES works for them to fully understand the inefficiencies and errors that occur due to non-integrated systems. The IT costs and operational costs will need to be factored out (estimated) over the long term.

Next, identify the long-term cost associated with migrating the systems to a new approach. Consider the incremental approach with the ability to quit at any point and still gain value. Suppose the organization chooses to go to a full implementation of a 3D ES. In that case, the costs will be significant, especially considering that the organization will still be incurring all the existing costs while it is making the transition. Having said that, the long-term IT costs should reduce dramatically, and the organization should experience cost reductions due to gains in efficiency.

The organization will also experience intangible benefits because of the transition. For example, it could improve decision-making as a result of more timely and accurate information or being able to fully leverage AI for the organization.

In the end, you will need to show the return on investment for making such a change. For some organizations, it may not be the right time and they may need to wait until the cost of transitioning goes down. The challenge with that option is that if their competition makes the transition first, it could put them at a disadvantage.

7.1.4 Developing the strategic plan

The strategic plan will detail how the organization will transform from the old paradigm to the new. It will describe each of the incremental steps identified above, review the progress, and assess improvement/challenges after each step. If the organization intends to proceed to a full 3D ES, the strategic plan will lay out the tactics for accomplishing it and the scope and budget for each envisioned 3D ES.

7.1.5 Stakeholders buy-in

Business managers/owners and their users benefit from the systems. We worked with these stakeholders to identify business issues associated with non-integrated systems. Now, we need to update them with a more comprehensive vision of how 3D ESs will work and the anticipated benefits. The project cannot proceed unless the business stakeholders buy into the new paradigm. Therefore, their support is critical.

7.1.6 Executive buy-in

In this book, you have everything necessary to present a proposal to the executive to get their buy-in for the strategic plan. The executive must understand why the current approach to systems is failing, why we need to change it, and what benefits we should expect to see, both short- and long-term. The executive will need to be well versed with the program, process, and fundamental concepts to convince a board that this is the right plan.

7.1.7 Conceptual design

The next step is to expand on the vision to produce a conceptual design. It will provide information on deliverables such as:

- A diagram that shows the key 3D ESs and how they will communicate.

- A description of the scope by the 3D ESs.

- A description of the organization of the 3D ESs by subnet.

- A description of how to share master data among 3D ESs.

- A description of how to share data with external entities.

- A description of how to share common functionality among 3D ESs.

- A full description of anticipated benefits.

It will be important for all stakeholders to understand and support the organization's target conceptual design.

7.2 Creating the enterprise data dictionary

7.2.1 Introduction

This is the first phase in moving toward 3D ESs. Given that systems already exist, it involves building the enterprise data dictionary by reverse engineering existing systems. During this effort, you will be able to reveal the challenges with using Software as a Service (SaaS) or cloud computing. You will discover that not all vendors reveal their data models or make it easy to extract data from their systems. After all, they don't want you to become independent of their lucrative long-term contracts. At any rate, you will need to create a dictionary that represents the data in your system(s). Below are the anticipated steps for creating the dictionary.

7.2.2 Define the sequence to reverse engineer

You need to plan out the sequence of systems to be reverse-engineered. Determine which systems or registries are most desirable to update or replace. For example, if an updated oil and gas well registry was highly desirable as a goal, then the critical oil and gas systems would be the first systems to be reverse engineered.

7.2.3 Download industry models

You will go to a 3D ES website and provide parameters for your industry and the systems you intend to create. The website will then provide you with core models extended on standard models containing business functions that align with the systems you intend to automate. (For information on who maintains this website, refer to section **Error! Reference source not found..**)

7.2.4 Reverse engineer systems

The process starts with capturing metadata about the columns within database tables for a given system. If you are fortunate, there will be a data dictionary either as a document or built into the system. With SQL databases, you can extract much of the information you need from the internal SQL dictionary. Next, you need to discern and identify tables that are capturing data of interest compared to tables that are merely working tables, system tables, or temporary tables. These latter tables are not of the same interest and do not need the same level of attention.

For each database table and column, specify information about the physical table name along with the column's name, description, format, and business rules. At this point, you will also identify the primary key columns. For foreign key columns, you will capture the columns involved (e.g., concatenated fields) in the foreign key and the table it references. From a table perspective, you will identify a description of the table and the type of table. The types of tables that you will encounter are:

- Data (master and transactional).

- System (internal tables for the system).

- Temporary (e.g., working).

- Reporting data.

- Reference table (contains many classification sub-tables held in a single table).

You only need to capture detailed metadata for data tables and reference tables. In the future, tools will be available to assist with this task. The tools will access a repository of metadata for systems that have been reverse engineered and will use machine learning to quickly reverse engineer your systems and produce the dictionary or glossary of terms. A business glossary lists business terms and their definitions and is usually intended for enterprise leaders. A data dictionary is usually a dataset in the form of a table, and a list of its fields and meanings and uses of those fields. The purpose of both a data dictionary and business glossary are to avoid different companies or departments using different terms for the same thing in a company.

7.2.5 Translate foreign keys

For master tables, we define how to translate foreign keys. For example, the translation for a GL Account ID on a GL Entry could be the reference number for the GL Account and a GL Account Description. The translation for a contact ID could be the name of the contact.

7.2.6 Classify metadata

Next, we apply a common classification system to all data tables and column names. This is known as a taxonomy, a scheme of classification, especially a hierarchical classification, in which things are organized into groups or types. The classification system has two main purposes. First, it helps to inventory the data so that we can analyze all data for a given subject. Second, it helps to see the duplication of data between systems, and this becomes the process of understanding which system has the gold standard (accurate and reliable data) for a given column.

For table classifications, it is best to classify them in a hierarchical classification scheme starting with broad category names and working down to greater detail. For example, all tables related to wells would be prefixed by "well".

Once again, tools in the future will use machine learning to evaluate your dictionary and classify the bulk of your metadata automatically, leaving you to deal with the exceptions.

7.2.7 Identify and generate common keys

To compare one system to the next, it will be necessary to define common keys. For example, suppose an organization has many systems that manage well data. In that case, it will be useful to have a common key created for wells (called a Unique Well Identifier, or UWI) that must be created consistently for all primary and foreign keys related to "wells". This virtual column will be created after consolidating data in the next step.

7.2.8 Consolidate data

For this step, you will need to export the data from existing systems into text files in a comma-delimited format. Then, built-in utilities will generate a database and import the data into the database's structures.

7.2.9 Report on data

The built-in utilities will programmatically generate views showing data from various systems using a common language. For example, in an oil and gas system, all tables that contain well data would be called "Well" and well status would be called "WellStatus" regardless of referencing system.

In addition, you use the common key (from step 7.2.7) to analyze existing data. This will allow you to create queries that join data from one system to another. For example, it could be comparing common attributes such as "well status" or joining master data in one system to transactional data in another.

The common key can also be the basis for creating a query engine for analyzing data. For example, we created a query engine based on the dictionary that returned data from all systems where a particular well, "UWI", was encountered. We could narrow this query down as follows:

- Show wells based on some portion of the UWI (such as all wells in an area).

- Show well data based on some portion of the classification of the data (For example, Well% would show data about wells but would also include Well Volume because it was prefixed by Well. Likewise, %Volume would show any data related to Volumes so Well Volumes would be included.

- Filter data by system to limit data to a particular system.

7.2.10 Streamline metadata

The purpose of the previous step is to have users mine all that data to better understand the applied classifications. If classifications are incorrect for columns and/or tables, then they could be updated and corrected, and the views regenerated. This is typically done by a business data steward.

7.2.11 Review status

You have successfully reverse-engineered systems and built a data dictionary at this point in the project. You will also have created software to mine the data to refine the dictionary's definitions. The dictionary will be a valuable resource for collecting knowledge about data in the form of metadata.

The organization can suspend further work on the project or continue to the next point. The ability to do this represents an incremental benefit since the organization gains value for each completed phase while retaining the ability to suspend activities after any phase.

7.3 Creating the registry systems

7.3.1 Introduction

The first step is the hardest when it comes to creating a large ES. Certainly, a big bang approach of developing the entire system in one project will not work. There is too much work and too much risk to such an endeavor. Instead, you will gain experience by creating registry systems first. A registry system manages data about one of the key subject areas. Examples of registries include a contact registry, fixed asset registry, land registry, an oil and gas well registry, etc.

You will need to create registries in a sequence to maintain referential integrity. For example, you may want to start with an oil and gas well registry, but it depends on data from other registries, such as the contact registry. You can start with a contact registry because it will have the least dependence on other registries. This section will use a contact registry as an example.

7.3.2 Define requirements

Contact data exists in every system. You will find data for contacts such as staff, suppliers, customers, and partners. The dictionary will help you to identify all data in all systems that deal with contacts. You will need to work with each business area to further elaborate on rules related to validating data about contacts. You will also be defining rules for record governance because not every business area can update every contact.

The goal of the contact registry in this phase of development is to consolidate all data about contacts in one place so that it can be communicated to other systems when contact information changes. As such, create interface requirements with the key systems. Some systems may be able to be updated through direct database updates, others with calls to APIs, and a few may have no interface and need to be updated manually.

Another option is creating a contact registry continually populated with data conversion scripts. The challenge will be to constantly deal with new duplicate contacts where the same contact is added in many different systems.

7.3.3   Extend core models to meet specific needs

We complete the process of creating the initial 3D ES database in this step. We extend the core model to include all the attributes that need to be managed by the new 3D ES. First, attributes that the core model covers are from the current system attributes to the core model attributes. For example, attributes related to contacts will be mapped to the attributes in the contact model. You will likely encounter attributes from many systems that map to the same attribute in the core model. For example, you may have many attributes that relate to the address attributes in many systems. The data conversion process will deal with these situations.

The process for creating new tables based on old ones is quite simple. It involves copying the attributes from the existing model to the new one and establishing the link from the old attribute to the new one. Once the copy is done, the table and column names can be changed to align with the naming conventions of the new paradigm.

The final step is to map the data in the model back to the requirements. If we need to include new attributes to meet business requirements, then the model will need to be extended to include those attributes. Everything about the new attributes can be defined, including the table containing the column, column name, data type, length (and decimals if applicable), business-friendly name, foreign key table (if it is a foreign key), nullability, and default value.

7.3.4 Generate the database

A utility is available that will take the completed dictionary from a spreadsheet and populate a staging database. Then the utility will run validations to ensure that the dictionary passes all integrity tests. After passing all integrity tests, the next utility runs, creating the database based on the definitions in the dictionary.

7.3.5 Convert the data

After creating the database, the next step populates the database based on the old database to the new mapping. The mapping deals with the following situations:

- **Splitting data from one table into two or more tables in the new system.** For example, a system may have contact and address data on the same record, but in the new system, contact data is on one record and address data is on another.

- **Consolidating data from multiple tables into one table in the new model.** For example, the new paradigm model consolidates supertype records for fixed assets in one table and data specific to subtypes in another. For example, we will see a vehicle have a supertype table for the generic asset information and a subtype table for the vehicle data.

- **Consolidating duplicate master data across multiple systems.** It is common to see the same master data duplicated across multiple systems. This process consolidates this data and converts all the primary key and foreign key references to the new 3D primary key format.

- **Setting up temporal (time-sensitive) data.** You will find that systems will have different conventions for managing time-sensitive data. This process deals with converting this data to a common convention so that all data can be dealt with consistently.

- **Converting reference tables to individual tables.** 3D ESs do not group any classification tables into a single table. Instead, each set of records in a reference table will be set up as their own reference table. This process deals with separating reference tables into their own tables.

- **Converting primary keys and foreign keys to the new 3D primary key format.** This process takes your existing primary keys and converts them to the new 3D primary key format. Then it takes the 3D primary key and uses it to assign foreign keys in all places where it is referenced.

7.3.6 Cleanse the data

The next step is verifying business rules for foreign key references, data constraints, and unique constraints. Utilities accomplish this by reading the data dictionary for business rules and exposing conditions that violate business rules. Errors detected will either be corrected in the source system, or we add business rules to a manual conversion step to cleanse the data. The manual conversion step also deals with any data conversion steps that the automated data conversion cannot accommodate.

7.3.7 Generate integrity constraints

After cleaning the data, the next step in the process begins. This step programmatically generates data integrity constraints on the database, such as foreign key constraints, null constraints, and unique constraints.

7.3.8 Generate views

Next, we programmatically generate views for browsing data. This process generates views based on user-friendly names for attributes. It will include both the foreign key column and the foreign key translation column for master data. For example, if it was a programmatically generated view for GL journal entries, it would include the foreign key column for the GL Account ID and the reference number and description for the GL Account. The columns in the view appear based on data from the data dictionary so that data looks correct in the views.

7.3.9   Scramble data

We are still in the process of creating the registry systems, so the next step in the process is to create software to scramble all personal and identifiable information. This means that the data will have to be scrambled on both the master record and transaction records, especially if it is copied from the master record to the transaction record.

The process starts with separating the name and its components (first name, middle name, etc.), birthdate, identification information (SINs), and address data. Then an algorithm is used to scramble all components so that a contact record will have randomized components for first name, middle name, birthdate, etc. We then move to the transactional data and perform string replacements. This makes the data look realistic but will have no meaning or correlation to the original records. When users begin system testing, eliminating the data scrambling step allows users to compare converted data to live data.

7.3.10 Generate the system

This phase involves using the metadata in the dictionary to generate parameters for online forms (browse, search, and edit) in the system. The system will also be able to add standard Create, Read, Update, and Delete (CRUD) menu options plus menu options for drilling down from master records to detail records. Likewise, if detail records tightly

358 • Fire, Water, Earth, Air, and Data

link to the master record, it can create forms with tabs (e.g., a contact form with a tab for the contact's addresses).

These definitions will supplement the definitions that already exist in the core system. For example, the core system already includes all the forms necessary to maintain information about contacts, finances, and assets (among others).

We create the custom forms after the base forms have been generated based on the dictionary. This process is for forms that are more complex than what can be generated by the automated process, but not so complex that custom programming is required. The last step in the process will be to create the forms that require custom programming.

7.3.11 Refine

This phase involves refining the data dictionary and forming parameters to deal with errors and extending the system to deal with new functional requirements. Users can see the forms with live data populated in them. This will help validate their requirements and validate that the data conversion worked properly. The data conversion process will be regularly re-run to generate a new database that contains fresh data and conforms to the updated business rules in the data dictionary.

7.4   Developing operational systems

Once sufficient registry systems are in place, the team can create operational systems. Operational systems are there to perform specific business functions. Examples of operational systems include those established for managing finances, processing claims, and managing inventory.

Over time, new paradigm third-party providers of commercial off-the-shelf systems (COTS) will create modules to perform common business functions for specific industries such as oil and gas, car manufacturers, etc. In the meantime, organizations will need to create these modules themselves with the help of consultants.

The process for creating operational systems will be much the same process as developing registry systems. Teams extend the dictionary to include existing systems that manage data in the same subject area within scope.

After updating the enterprise data dictionary, we classify it into subject categories. Next, the new model will be created by downloading the appropriate core models from the 3D ES foundation and mapping the old data onto the new model. The final step will generate the conversion script from the data dictionary. Data specialists manage the data dictionary throughout the development process and will continually refine it to support data requirements from the business analysis.

Tools will be available at every step to minimize the team's efforts in performing any tasks related to creating the new model. Examples of such tools are:

- Tools to reverse engineer systems, create new models, and map data from the existing to the new models.

- Tools to generate data conversion scripts to convert data from the old to the new system.

- Tools to generate forms.

7.5 Summary

Generating a system will take lots of effort, but it will be considerably easier to create and maintain than systems under the old paradigm. One of the key benefits of how the new paradigm approach ESs, is that data conversions are one of the first steps in the development process rather than one of the last. This will help developers work with live data and minimize the effort to generate test cases. It will also help users test by seeing recent live data in their test systems. In addition, the entire function evaluates and confirms conversion processes early in the development phase so that they are fully tested when the system goes live.

Creating systems will happen one by one, reducing risk and facilitating incremental progress. The organization should be able to suspend the process of creating the complete 3D ES at any time and still receive value from the systems generated to that point in time.

8 Release Management

Whether a system is in development or production, we will need to manage software releases. The development of a new system will kick off with a new release assigned a release number. After development and testing, the release will move through various test environments. The first test environment could be for the specific 3D ES, and a subsequent test environment could be for all 3D ESs working together. Eventually, the release will make it to production. When a release moves from development to testing, a new release number will be set up for the developers.

A key part of creating a new release is managing the parameters stored in the database, which drives how the system works. For example, these parameters control what menu options are available and how search, browse, and edit forms look.

3D ESs can accommodate the incremental release strategy. With each new release, a new database will be created with that release number. When the release is complete, the build master can automatically generate a database script that will represent all of the inserts, updates, and deletes done to the parameter tables as a part of the release.

We combine the script with other database scripts, such as function updates, views, and database conversion scripts. We also include source code updates for custom modules.

We combine all this into a package that can be applied to any environment. Special features are built into 3D primary keys so that if we add a new parameter record in one environment, we can use the build script to add it to any other environment without ever generating any colliding 3D primary keys.

9 Recruiting and Educating Resources

9.1 Introduction

Many roles will exist when creating 3D ESs. Some of these roles will be similar to those in the industry today with some variation, and others will be new. This section describes each of the roles that will be required. In any major change, you always require senior management/executive sponsorship, steering committees, and change management to be involved. You can always start the 3D ES approach as a pilot if the risks appear too big for the organization to fully buy-in.

When the team fills a role, it is important that the incumbent or new hire fully subscribes to the 3D ES model. If they are steadfast in old paradigm approaches to systems or their vision for the solution is considerably different, they will diminish the worth or value of the team's effort. You need team members that fully buy in, understand the approach, and are committed to making it succeed. Resources should be required to have some form of 3D ES education, pass interviews that verify their understanding and support for the process, and have ideas on improvements. To illustrate this point further, consider Tesla. Tesla does not hire engineers that believe that the hydrogen cell is the way of the future, no matter how brilliant and experienced they are. Just like Tesla, 3D ES projects will succeed based on teams striving for the same goal. Resources will likely take on one or more roles. Here is a description of each of the necessary roles:

- **Enterprise architects.** Enterprise architects will work alone or as a team to formulate the vision for an organization's 3D ES. They will then extend that vision into a more detailed conceptual design. Then they will pass a defined scope of the 3D ES modules to the business analysts and data architects to define business and data requirements. The enterprise architects will also define common modules that must be created and shared among 3D ESs.

- **Project manager.** The project manager will be responsible for managing 3D ES projects based on the scope of 3D ESs provided by the architect. They will develop the project plan, prepare earned value reports, and report status to the project sponsor.

- **Business analysts.** Business analysts will work with subject matter experts to define system requirements and prepare specifications. Business analysts will have specialties in business areas. For example, a business analyst specializing in finance modules will have different skills than someone specializing in enterprise resource planning.

- **Data architects.** Data architects will be intimately familiar with the core data structures and understand how to augment the structures to meet the specific needs of the business. In addition, they will be responsible for creating the enterprise data dictionary and the associated data models based on the requirements defined by the business analysts. They will map the data from existing systems into the new database. Once they complete this task, they will pass it on to the database administrator and data conversion specialist to complete the conversion.

- **Security specialists.** Security specialists will work on the project to ensure that all security protocols are followed.

- **Data conversion specialists.** Data conversion specialists will be experts at finishing off the automated data conversion with any manual conversion that may be necessary.

- **Database administrators.** Database administrators will be responsible for ensuring that the database is correctly created. They will also ensure that it is properly secured and tuned for optimal performance. The tuning task will involve monitoring the database for resource-intensive processes and adjusting indexes to optimize performance.

- **Master data specialists.** Master data specialists will examine the organization's master data to ensure it is properly shared among 3D ESs.

- **Integration specialists.** Integration specialists will create the integrations to the old paradigm (legacy) systems using stub systems.

- **Framework specialists.** Framework specialists will work solely with the application frameworks. The application frameworks control the features of the interface(s) developed for users, how the application controls security, and how the front-end moves data back and forth to the databases. Application frameworks will exist for all environments, including web, desktop, and mobile devices.

- **Database script developers.** The database script developers will specialize in creating complex database functions. These developers will know how to create complex routines in the finance system for billing processes or develop complex routines for ESs.

- **Data exchange specialists.** Data exchange specialists will be experts at defining custom rules for importing data into systems. Examples of custom rules are kicking off workflow processes when certain types of data updates are received.

- **Application developers and business automation specialists.** Application developers will specialize in developing custom forms outside the framework's capabilities. The business automation specialists will work with subject matter experts trained in and efficient at creating interfaces through the user interface engine. This includes developing automated processes quickly to suit the rapidly changing business needs. The business automation specialists can go outside the application framework and code special forms as required. As time goes on, the capabilities of the application framework will increase, and there will be less need to go outside the application framework to address users' requirements.

- **Report developers.** Report developers will specialize in creating all types of reports based on business requirements. Self-service analytics is one of the key requirements of managers and business leaders. This will be easier to provide within the 3D ES environment.

- **Testers.** Testers will be responsible for developing test scripts and test cases. They will perform both system and integration tests.

- **Build masters.** Build masters will specialize in creating new builds for testing and moving updates for the system from one environment to another. The build master will ensure all source code and related script files are managed in a source code repository.

- **Data warehouse specialist.** The data warehouse specialist will aggregate data from all 3D ESs into a single repository for reporting. They will develop reports and dashboards for management. Increased data accuracy and quality will provide for better data warehouse analytics and management confidence in the reports they receive.

- **Data scientists.** Data scientists will use data in the data warehouse to develop machine learning and AI routines. The data scientists will do very little if any data cleansing.

- **Data governance and data stewards.** Data Governance provides the charter and mandate for data stewards to actively monitor data, to achieve a common understanding between business users who own the data and recommend policy for the organization (naming conventions, changes in size, description, etc.). Data governance also specifies access to data and who owns the record and assuring conformance with government and international regulations for data protection and privacy. In 3D ES we aid data governance by providing a record ownership and transfer model.

10 Governing the New Paradigm

10.1 Introduction

The 3D ES foundation that performs key functions to coordinate sharing among enterprise architects is at the hub of the new paradigm. The 3D ES foundation will be a non-profit entity that is either a new organization or an existing organization with new responsibilities. The 3D ES foundation will perform the following functions.

10.2 Maintaining the 3D ES website

A 3D ES website will need to be maintained that provides access to core data structures, the 3D ES framework, and education resources.

10.3 Governing the core data structures

The core data structures are small, powerful, and integrated structures common to every ES. They encompass data for contacts, finances, assets, products, contracts, and other categories. The core data structures also encompass the administrative tables that capture the user interface's parameter information. This includes menu hierarchies, security groups, form definitions (search, browse, edit), process definitions, audit history, data governance, and others.

All core structures will have strict naming conventions, with attributes specified in long form with an abbreviation engine that consistently applies abbreviations to create abbreviated names.

There will need to be a technical committee that accepts ideas for updating and extending the core models. The core models will not often change because the nature of core models is that it represents the common occurring attributes we see in any business. We will extend core models to new subject areas like manufacturing or retail.

10.4 Managing the master data exchange server

We will need to manage the public master data exchange server. It is a Postgres database accessed from subnet servers, which keeps track of systems, subnet servers, and master data packages waiting to be read by a subnet server. It will also keep track of governance exceptions. The 3D ES foundation will host this server.

10.5 Application framework specifications

The organization will maintain specifications for features required in any new application frameworks that organizations produce. Also, test scripts will verify that the application frameworks are functioning as expected. The 3D ES foundation will maintain version control of the framework specifications.

10.6 Managing specifications/test scripts for enterprise definition tools

There will be a number of tools necessary for analyzing, designing, and creating 3D ESs, including:

10.6.1 Enterprise data dictionary tool

The enterprise data dictionary tool will be the one that connects to the 3D ES foundation data dictionary. This tool will help reverse engineer, document, and design new databases based on the core data structures. Other features of the enterprise data dictionary tool include:

- Checking database integrity (including foreign keys).

- Generating views that assist with the analysis of data across all systems, based on terminology common across all databases.

- Connecting to the 3D ES foundation dictionary to assist with mapping and transforming scripts to the new database.

- Generating conversion scripts that automate the migration of data to the new database.

10.6.2 Menu, form, and process definition tool

These tools will be available to business analysts and developers for defining menu structures and designing forms for search, browse, and edit. It will also allow processes and dashboards to be defined. Various providers will develop the tools, but the definitions will be stored in tables according to the conventions of the data dictionary. Furthermore, data will be created with 3D IDs and definitions about how it is governed in the same way that data is governed overall.

10.7 Training and certifications

The organization must establish a training program and deliver it to architects. It will also need to certify resources. A process much like the ISO 9001 quality management approach is required for 3D ES proponents and followers. This process will cover the training, certifying, auditing, and validating of those organizations that have signed up for implementing 3D ESs.

10.8 Consulting

Consulting services will be involved in training, certifying, auditing, validating, and assisting projects with developing their data models and creating their systems.

11 Conclusion

If you have made it this far in the book, congratulations! That is a lot of material. We hope that you have found value in the material and can clearly see the vision for the 3D ES. We hope it has become clear that we have hit the wall in terms of what we can accomplish with the old paradigm approach to ES software. The challenge is with all the advances in software development tools, we are creating silo systems faster than ever, which only exasperates the problem.

The old paradigm approach involves creating systems designed in silos. When we attempt to integrate these systems, we realize we cannot integrate them with the other silo systems to a large extent. Once an organization cannot take the pain of many disparate systems, it turns to an ES vendor to implement a large system that encompasses more of the business functions.

Implementing a large ES can be very expensive and ties the organization to the vendor with little ability to change. When we step past large organizations to conglomerates, the issues grow bigger. With the old paradigm approach, we cannot create systems for all the entities within a conglomerate and then fully integrate all the systems. Instead, the old paradigm forces us to put all the functionality in a single monolithic system and then implement row-level security (which has performance implications) to stop one department from viewing another department's data.

The larger the systems get, the higher the costs and associated risks. However, instead of going up linearly, they go up exponentially because each new function added to the scope needs to be integrated with previous functions implemented.

As architects, we intuitively know the problem has a solution, but it will involve stepping back and formulating a new approach designed from the ground up with the end in mind. Of course, there will be a tremendous amount of effort to recreate all of the systems that are currently in place. That said, systems do not last forever and eventually need to be replaced. Replacing these systems using old paradigm approaches is difficult. Rearchitecting and recreating the same functionality over and over is a waste of time. Integrating and aggregating data for hundreds of silo systems is a futile effort that bogs down our industry.

We believe the 3D ES paradigm is the solution to address these issues. However, whatever the solution is, it will have to begin with the first four principles identified in this book. Namely, we will have to create systems based on a core data model and build out from those core data models with industry-specific models. We will need to change how we identify data with a new type of 3D primary key assigned once a record is created and never changes no matter how many systems it appears. We will need to control governance for updating records, so we always know where the book of record exists. We will need to have built-in mechanisms that allow us to transfer data between systems and then have those systems react to the incoming data.

The fifth principle of 3D ESs is to build systems based on a framework that operates much like a web browser. This principle is critical for achieving all the benefits of a 3D ES, but it is not mandatory. For example, systems could be custom-built without a framework for the front-end layers that connect to the back-end 3D ES utilities.

At any rate, this book intends to kick off the process for the new paradigm. It is not the last deliverable on this subject. We need experts in all areas to dovetail their work into this core. For example, experts in microservice, master data management, data governance, security, enterprise software architecture, data warehousing, artificial intelligence, industry data models, and data modeling can all build on this body of work to help the software industry achieve the same great productivity gains we have seen in other areas of the IT Industry like hardware.

The new paradigm will be especially transformative for countries that adopt it and support it with legislation, education, and funding. Of course, there will be challenges for early adopters, as there always will be. But early adopters will have the most influence in shaping the new paradigm in ES software.

Countries that fully adopt the approach will see commerce and government performed at breakneck speed where data is only ever entered once and leveraged many times across all types of organizations. These countries will win the race for leveraging artificial intelligence for business systems.

The same applies to large companies plagued with all the issues that a diversity of system provide when you have a plethora of silo systems. When these companies realize that the old paradigm approach to systems is never going to work, they will transition to rethinking how they create their systems.

The question is who is going to make that decision for them. Will IT resources be forward-thinking enough to support a new approach to ES software, or will they wait until their executives see their competition jumping ahead and come asking questions as to why the competitor company systems are more flexible than their own.

What will you do if you are one of those IT resources? We hope you see the dire need for change in our industry and recognize this as a good step in the right direction.

APPENDIX A

Applying 3D ES to Data Warehouses and Data Lakehouses

A.1 Introduction

This appendix discusses how the new paradigm's use of core models, 3D primary keys, and governance will change how we create data warehouses and data lakehouses. First, we discuss the challenges of creating data warehouses for structured data and then discuss how creating data warehouses in the new paradigm will be different. Finally, we cover how the new paradigm will increase our ability to connect structured, unstructured, and analog data in data lakehouses.

A.2 The data warehouse challenge

With today's approach to enterprise systems, organizations can spend many hours aggregating data from different systems into a data warehouse for reporting. The more systems, the more challenging the process. It is extremely challenging due to all the limitations of the old paradigm approach. The old paradigm approach involves creating systems in silos. This approach starts with defining a scope of business functions to be automated and then creating a system to address the requirements. In the process, the team will create a database based on their preferences.

They will decide how to structure the data (e.g., whether to use recursive structures) and choose naming conventions for tables and attributes. The team will decide how to use primary keys. Some will choose incremented integer keys, others will choose composite keys, and others will choose GUIDs. In some cases, you will see all three in the same system.

Teams will also decide how to store temporal (time-sensitive) data. For example, some teams will duplicate all the data for each time series, others will keep track of temporal data by attribute, and others will date stamp data with start and end dates.

The resulting system will end up with a database that is unique as a fingerprint. The approach for creating systems is the same whether it is a custom system, a software as a service solution, or an ERP system.

When a team creates a data warehouse, it will need to reverse engineer the underlying databases and categorize the data by subject. The team will find for a given subject that there are a varied number of attributes about the subject in each system, so it will need to decipher which attributes are common. When the team finds an attribute like status, it will often run into a situation where each system has a different number of statuses that mean different things. For example, if the team finds an attribute for a staff member like employment status, the time reporting system, payroll system, and HR system all have different statuses.

To address this issue, the team must decide on an attribute-by-attribute basis on which system to source the attribute. This causes challenges as well. For example, if you were pulling data about home addresses, you can't take the city, address, and postal code from one system and the phone number from another because the addresses may be out of sync.

The next issue is primary keys. With each system having different primary keys for the same data, the team will need to assign a primary key and cross reference every primary key from every system for the same data. This is challenging enough, but what happens when data is structured differently. For example, many systems may keep addresses for a contact, but it is difficult to correlate an address from one system to the next and be assured it is the same address record.

The last main issue is record governance. If multiple systems maintain data about the same subject, then which system is the correct source of that data? For example, if you aggregated contact data from many different systems, which system will you trust as the correct version?

The issue of record governance can also become more granular. For example, an oil and gas company may have well data spread across many different systems. You might trust the location data from one system but the well status from another. The issue with combining this data is that it can be in different states of timeliness.

In the end, we spend countless hours trying to aggregate data from many different systems into a data warehouse.

A.3 How the new paradigm manages data

The new paradigm approach is architected from the bottom up to deal with integration issues. The new paradigm creates data structures based on core structures that manage the common data to all organizations. These structures are designed to be easily extended to track data unique to an industry and further extended to track data unique to an organization.

The core structures set patterns for naming conventions. In addition, the core structures have embedded features for tracking temporal (time sensitive) data and features for tracking change history (audit logging).

Using core structures is not a new concept. ERP vendors, as an example, do not change their underlying structures for managing contacts and finances for each new industry they support. Instead, they build on their core structures to accommodate the unique requirements of a given industry.

The next key feature of the new paradigm that simplifies data extracting, transforming, and loading into warehouses is 3D primary keys. In the new paradigm, when a record is created in any system, it is assigned a 3D primary key containing two components. The first component identifies the system that created the 3D primary key, and the second contains a unique ID for that record within the table where the record was created. For example, if a system was assigned an ID of 1312, then the first record it would create would have an ID of 1312-1. The next record would be 1312-2.

The two components of the 3D primary key allow us to create data in one system and move it to another without worrying about colliding with the same key in the destination system.

The next key principle of the new paradigm is record governance. Record governance says that only one system can own the governance for a given record. By default, when a system creates a record, it automatically governs the record. But if the need arises, the governance can be transferred to another system. For example, with a membership system, a member may be created in Alberta, but they may move to Ontario, where the governance transfers to Ontario. This means all entities, including the Alberta entity, would now go to the Ontario entity to get the most current version of the record.

The last key principle is data transference. It states that we need to have a methodology supported by an automated process for transferring and synchronizing master data between entities. It states that we will have systems that publish master data and systems that can subscribe to it. Data can be as simple as a single record or a grouping of records. For example, suppose we were sharing access to a contract record. In that case, it could be the contract header record or it could also include subsidiary records that identify the contract participants or contract terms.

Data transference allows for record structures to be modified by either the publisher or subscriber. It takes care of transferring master data when initially subscribing. The new paradigm system includes built-in change history (audit logging), so whenever a subscribed record gets updated, the updates are automatically broadcasted to all subscribers.

All these principles working together form the basis of being able to transfer data between systems. We can easily aggregate data from all systems because we are now using consistent data structures, have primary keys consistent across all systems, and have record governance so we know which system to trust and share the same master data because of a formal record transference procedure.

Teams will be educated on architecting and creating systems using the new paradigm methods. They will no longer create systems by function (like payroll, HR, time reporting) and will instead create systems to meet the needs of a locality (like a department, region, or retail outlet). Business functions like payroll, HR, and time reporting will become common business functions to share in an open-source method between systems.

A.4 Creating the data warehouse

The new paradigm includes a utility that automatically generates a data warehouse based on data from all the business entities that have 3D ES systems. The data warehouse will contain every table and attribute from each 3D ES system.

This utility is possible because of 3D primary keys, record governance and master data management utilities.

The utility can also be expanded to eliminate duplicate records that were accidentally added in the separate business systems.

All data in the warehouse will use the 3D primary keys in the source databases.

The data warehouse will be accessible from data, system and time dimensions.

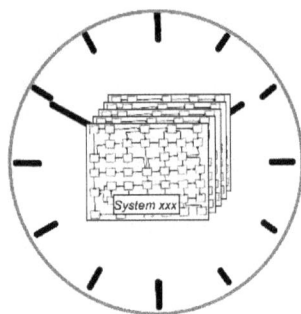

In addition, data lineage is critical, and the system will include a complete change history (audit log) that shows all the changes made to the data since its creation, along with who made the changes.

A.5 Creating the data lakehouse

There are three data types in the data lakehouse: structured, unstructured, and analog. Structured data represents the data from the data warehouse. Unstructured data represents data such as emails, contracts, and call center logs. Analog data is generated automatically from automated processes such as IoT.

The three types of data are connected using universal common connectors. The most basic universal common connectors are geographical location, time, and dollars. Data can also be connected using ids. For example, in manufacturing, we can capture a unit ID in all three types of data. Then we can connect structured, unstructured, and analog data based on the unit ID for analysis.

The new paradigm will build on this concept by extending ids to also include a subject ID. The data dictionary identifies all the subjects within the database. Subjects are equivalent to entities within the data dictionary. Examples of subjects/entities are contacts, assets, locations, or any other type of entity within the database.

Entities in the dictionary are identified with the new type of 3D primary key, including the system that originally created the entity and a record ID. For example, the core model includes an entity for contract data. It also includes all the other entities you would commonly find in organizations like assets, GL accounts, GL cost centers, locations, and contracts. The core entities are extended for industries and organizations to meet specific needs. The data dictionary presents a taxonomy of the structured data you would find in an organization. It also identifies the ontology of how those taxonomies interrelate.

Each data entity in the data dictionary is identified by a 3D primary key that identifies the original system that created it and a unique record ID. Any data entities created as core data entities common to all organizations (like contacts, GL accounts, and cost centers), are identified by system ID zero. Any new entities created are identified by the system that created them. As a result of using the new type of 3D primary key, we can merge dictionaries from multiple entities.

When unstructured or analog data is recorded, we will capture the entity ID and the record ID. This will allow us to link data for any type of entity across structured, unstructured, and analog data.

For example, if we were manufacturing an item, we would include an item ID allowing us to connect structured, unstructured, and analogy data for the item. The item ID would include the entity ID from the data dictionary that described 'items'. It would also include the unique ID for the item.

Of course, we would not just be limited to manufactured items. In fact, we could capture data about any other type of entity in our dictionary by merely recording the entity ID from the dictionary plus the unique record ID of the item.

If we were recording data about a contract, it would be the ID of contract data from the dictionary plus the ID of the contract from the contract table.

There can be more than a thousand entities in a dictionary and this mechanism would allow any type of data to be uniquely identified across structured, unstructured, and analog data.

A.6 Summary

The new paradigm will simplify the process of aggregating data from many different systems into a data warehouse for reporting. It will accomplish this by creating systems based on core structures, using 3D primary keys that allow us to transfer data between systems without changing the keys, and by record governance, so we always know which system owns the correct version of a record.

The system will include a taxonomy of the structured data in an organization. This is captured in the data dictionary, which also includes an ontology of how that data interrelates.

The entity ID and record ID are recorded when capturing unstructured or analog data. As a result, we can create a data lakehouse that links all types of structured, unstructured, and analog data.

From Data Warehouse to Lakehouse, by Bill Inmon

Data can be organized in many ways:

- Applications
- Data marts
- Data warehouses
- Data lakehouses

It is easy when dealing with data to become overwhelmed with detail. Many details need to be understood, aligned, and organized. Furthermore, these details seem to be in constant motion. The classical way to understand data in whatever its form is through a data model.

In its simplest form, the data model is simply an abstraction of the data it represents. A data model is like a lighthouse on the ocean. The lighthouse serves to warn sailors of dangerous rocks and reefs. In addition, lighthouses can be used for navigation. And lighthouses are for everyone, including small ships, large ships, ocean liners, and row boats. It is a time-honored tradition to build data models to organize and understand data.

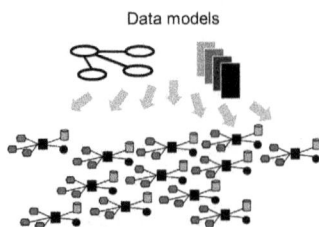

Data models

Figure B-1. There are two basic forms of a data model: classical and taxonomy. The classical data model serves to represent structured data. The classical data model is also called an entity/relationship diagram (ERD). The taxonomy serves to describe textual data.

B.1 Classical data models

So, what are the elements of a classical data model for structured data? They include:

- **Definition.** For example, customer may be defined as a person who has made a purchase. Conversely, if a person or organization has not made a purchase, that person is not a customer.

- **Name.** This can mean the name of the database, an attribute, an index, or other type of data.

- **Physical structure.** Characters, numerics, bit strings, or other.

- **Selection criteria.** What data was included/excluded for entrance to the set of data?

- **Calculation.** Some data requires a calculation, such as interest rates, monthly revenue, sales tax, etc.

The elements of a data model serve to define and depict the data for the many different communities that will need to access and use the data. So, who needs to use a classical structured data model? Many users, including:

- Programmers and developers who must work with the ongoing changes to the data,
- End user analysts who must use the data for the work they do,
- Management,
- Auditors

B.2 About text

But the classical data model only defines the organization's structured data. And in most organizations, the structured data of the organization only represents a small fraction of the data flowing through the corporation.

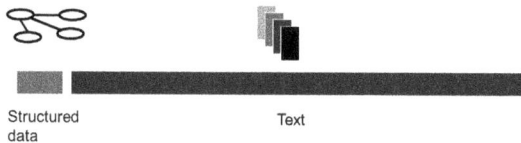

Structured data   Text

Figure B-2. The vast majority of the data flowing through the corporation is, in fact, the text that the corporation uses.

We find text in:

- Emails
- Advertisements
- Web pages

- Corporate contracts
- Medical records

B.3 Taxonomies and ontologies

The lighthouse for textual data is a structure called a taxonomy (categorization, classification) or an ontology (linked classifications, categorizations). Like the data model that serves as a lighthouse of structured data, the taxonomy serves as a lighthouse for textual data. A taxonomy is nothing more than a classification of like words. There are many taxonomies found in the world.

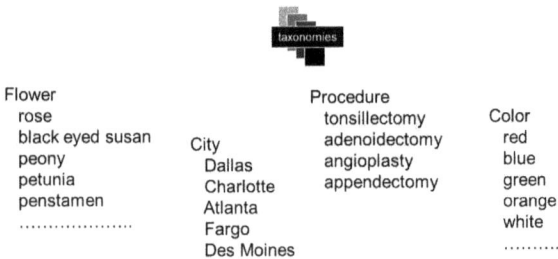

Flower		Procedure	Color
rose		tonsillectomy	red
black eyed susan	City	adenoidectomy	blue
peony	Dallas	angioplasty	green
petunia	Charlotte	appendectomy	orange
penstamen	Atlanta		white
....	Fargo		....
	Des Moines		

Figure B-3. All of the elements in a taxonomy are deeper descriptions of the same thing.

For example, if you had a taxonomy of cars that looked like:

Car

Porsche

Honda

Ford

Toyota

You would not have a taxonomy with:

Car
Porsche
Honda
Ford
Butter

Butter is not a further description of a car and does not fit with the other taxonomical descriptions. A taxonomy is related to an ontology. An ontology is nothing more than a group of taxonomies where there is a relationship between the different elements.

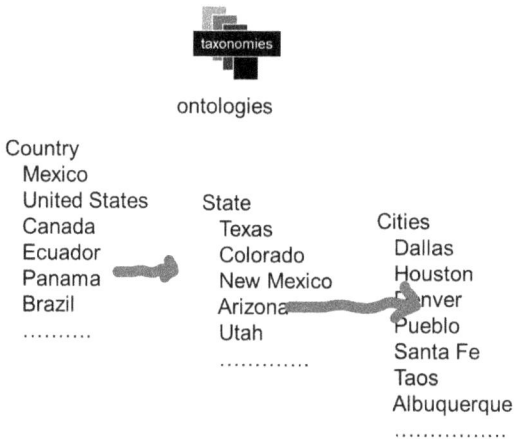

Figure B-4. There are three taxonomies: one for country, one for state, and one for city. There is an interrelationship between state and country and city and state. Together the three taxonomies form an ontology.

There are actually a lot of reasons why taxonomies are so useful for describing text. The primary reason is that in communicating, we use taxonomies without even knowing it. For example, if you had the sentence:

Kewal plays with his red Miata in Edmonton all the time.

The same sentence could be stated:

He drives his colorful sports car through a town in Canada frequently.

The two sentences say the same thing. But in the first sentence, there is much less classification than in the second sentence.

B.4 Data model versus taxonomy

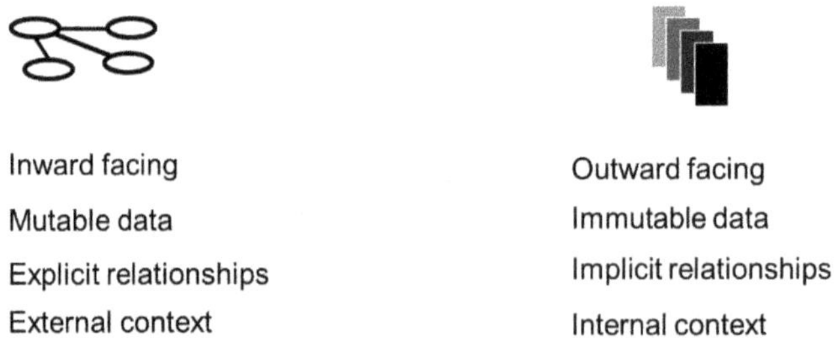

Inward facing
Mutable data
Explicit relationships
External context

Outward facing
Immutable data
Implicit relationships
Internal context

Figure B-5. While there are many similarities between the classical data model and taxonomies, there are nonetheless some significant differences.

One of the differences is that a data model is inward facing while a taxonomy is external facing. The data model serves to portray the internal working of the corporation. The taxonomy serves to portray the world external to the organization.

Another difference is the understanding that if structured data needs to be changed, a change is always possible. However, textual data cannot ever be changed. It may even be illegal to go back and restate textual data.

Yet another difference between the two types of models is in terms of their expression of structure. In structured data, the structure of the data is explicitly defined in the tables, attributes, and key/foreign key relationships. Those structures are defined at the moment of design and are explicitly stated in the design of the data. But with textual data and taxonomies, the interrelationships of the data are buried inside the physical structure of the data. It is then incumbent on the developer to bring out those relationships. This puts more of a burden on the developer in the world of textual analytics but is far more flexible than the explicit data structures found in a data model.

In the same vein, the context of structured data is explicitly found in the structure defined by the designer. But in textual data represented by a taxonomy, the context of data is found internally to the expressions of text.

In any case, the classical data model and the taxonomy/ontology set the stage for a deeper understanding of the data found in the corporation.

In this appendix, I provided a brief view of the various kinds of data and how one might organize it for analysis. You will find more guidance in my book by Technics Publications, *Building the Data Lakehouse*.

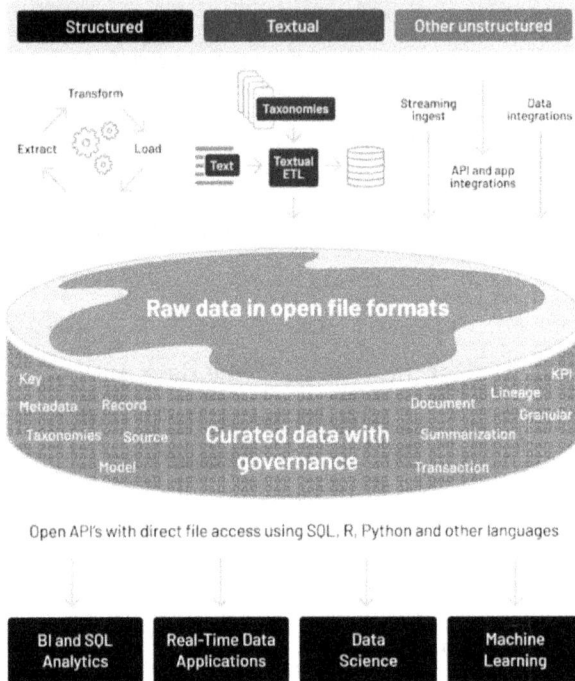

Figure B-6. To avoid turning your data lake into a swamp, you need to organize, categorize and classify your data before you load it. While data lakes are useful, the problem with data lakes is architectural. Often, extracting meaningful data from a data lake is difficult. A data lakehouse is a blend of data lake and data warehouse architecture techniques, where we can increase data quality, simultaneously providing for data lineage to be tracked and governed.

In the context of this current book with Blair Kjenner and Kewal Dhariwal, my concept of common connectors to organize and classify data is quite useful and fosters systems integration for data analytics. Universal Common Connectors such as geography, time, and dollar amount allow us to determine common data and perform meaningful analytics. In healthcare, common data relates to humans' medical treatments and vaccinations and whether the medicines and vaccinations worked and with the right effect

To do analytics, there must be some common data able to be linked in some manner. Without this common data, it is very difficult to identify and explore meaningful comparison.

The problem is that there may be no obvious, easy way for us to isolate common identifiers. 3D ESs and 3D primary keys provide a useful and efficient way for us to find the data we need and integrate it in the data lakehouse.

Proctor and Gamble (P&G) Example of 3D ES

I asked Blair about how 3D ES would work for as complex a system as I could imagine – that being one of the largest multinational companies in the world P&G, which has about 19 products generating over a US$1 Billion annually and owns many subsidiary operating companies. It is organized by product divisions and Brand managers and with geographical locations all over the world. His response below:

Here's how it could be accomplished using 3D Enterprise Systems:

1. Proctor and Gamble would create an industry layer that expanded on the core models. The industry layer would encompass data that was common across all their regions (Asia Pacific, Europe, Greater China, IMEA, LATAM, North America).

2. It would then populate the models with data that was common to all regions in a head office system. For example, the product table would be pre-populated with products common to all regions.

Likewise, GL Accounts, Activity types, Cost Centre Schemes and tens of other types of classification data would be prepopulated in the model.

3. Next, they would setup systems for each region and then would customize the data models to meet the unique needs of each region. If that region sold products that were unique to their region, then the product list setup in step 2 would be augmented with data that was unique to that region. Likewise, any of the other master data created in step 2 could be augmented for a given region.

4. Systems would then be setup for each country that rolled up to the regional systems. The systems for each country would be customized to meet the unique needs of that country. The country systems would inherit data from the regional systems and then extend it to meet its unique needs.

5. Head Office, Regional and Country systems would be fully functional systems to meet all business needs including contact management and finance and administration.

6. Master data would be defined at the head office level and then inherited and extended at both the regional and country level. Each entity could

maintain contact data for their own purpose but share contacts that they had in common.

7. The time dimension would apply to products and other kinds of data. For example, products come into existence and are eventually discontinued. The costs of the products also change over time.

8. All data could be aggregated from the head office system and regional systems for reporting.

   o Single Contact registry for all regions and head office

   o Aggregate all detailed financial records

   o Aggregate all product data which included products sold across each region plus products unique to a region.

   o Aggregate all activity data across all regions and head office. For example, if we had activities related to products for development and support that were initiated in the head office and regions, we would see them all aggregated in one place.

8. The time dimension would allow us to see product data that changed over time (among other types of temporal data)

9. The system dimension would allow us to see which system the data originated from (e.g. look at activity data and see which system created it.

10. The data dimension represents the core and industry data that we could analyze across the entire proctor and gamble product line

11. From a maintenance perspective, if a new product was created or changed, it would be automatically distributed to each system based on a hierarchical subscriber group. Likewise, if any other classification data changed (GL accounts, etc.) it would automatically be broadcast.

This is a very good example of the complexity that we can deal with. We can break down systems from head office to a region to a country and allow each system to be customized to meet the unique needs of a locality (like tax laws) and we have the ability to take data that is created in all the systems and aggregate it for reporting.

Index

functional, 14, 35, 47, 62, 114,
133, 134, 139, 142, 175, 268,
341, 358
functions, 3, 9, 38, 39, 50, 59, 62,
63, 92, 119, 126, 130, 139, 149,
155, 157, 159, 166, 171, 182,
205, 227, 257, 286, 287, 346,
359, 368, 371, 376, 377, 382,
387
GAADP. See Generally
Accepted Application
Development Principles
GAAP. See Generally Accepted
Accounting Principles
GADMP. See Generally
Accepted Data Management
Principles
Gartner, 22
General Ledger, 125, 232
Generally Accepted
Accounting Principles, 40,
69
Generally Accepted
Application Development
Principles, 69
Generally Accepted Data
Management Principles, 69
GL. See General Ledger
GL account number, 76, 166
Globally Unique Identifier, 77
gold standard, 25, 123, 227, 348
Google, 52
Gotterbarn, Don, 21
government, 3, 7, 10, 75, 97,
124, 131, 133, 134, 135, 136,
207, 324, 379
governor, 89, 91, 92, 93, 94, 96,
120, 149, 199, 211, 218, 222,
223, 224, 225, 226, 227

GUID. See Globally Unique
Identifier
Header Data, 100
healthcare, 1, 3, 15, 37, 38, 62,
102, 124, 125, 126, 127, 128,
207, 258, 401
healthcare worker, 124
Henderson, Debra, 21
hierarchical, 90, 98, 154, 165,
166, 167, 214, 218, 219, 221,
228, 236, 237, 252, 260, 267,
269, 273, 274, 276, 307, 348
Hoberman, Steve, 21
hospitals, 13, 125, 207, 218
HTML, 59, 107
ICCP, 21, 60
IEEE, 9, 21
import process, 208, 223, 225
incremented integer, 76, 77, 80,
81, 84, 158, 181, 382
industry model, 71, 72, 98
Inmon, Bill, 2, 21
integrated development
environment, 151
integration specialist, 368
javascript, 106
Jensen, Bradley, 21
journal entry, 70, 83, 149, 169,
184, 198, 231, 232, 235, 236,
237, 238, 239, 241, 242, 243,
244, 261, 269, 270, 275, 276,
278, 279, 284, 285, 286, 287,
288, 289, 290, 291, 292, 293,
294, 295, 323, 356
JSON, 157, 158, 202
key objectives, 58
key-value, 154, 156, 332
land registry, 134, 351
Lane, Greg, 21
Lloyd's of London, 29

www.ingramcontent.com/pod-product-compliance
Lightning Source LLC
Chambersburg PA
CBHW071537210326
41597CB00019B/3029